roach to the Manse in the wood.
The Gairn, the Black Briggie,
and the Manse Brae

Fording the Gairn,
near the Manse

Glen Gairn Church

Wedding Day – 24th July, 1914.
Dr. Mark Stewart Fraser and
Amy Stewart Fraser

# Roses
# in
# December

Also by Amy Stewart Fraser

*The Hills of Home*
*In Memory Long*
*Dae Ye Min' Langsyne?*

# Roses
# in
# December

## *Edwardian Recollections*

Amy Stewart Fraser

*God gave us Memory so that we might have roses in December*
J. M. Barrie

Routledge & Kegan Paul
London, Boston and Henley

*First published in 1981*
*by Routledge & Kegan Paul Ltd*
*39, Store Street, London WC1E 7DD,*
*9 Park Street, Boston, Mass. 02108, USA and*
*Broadway House, Newtown Road, Henley-on-Thames, Oxon RG9 1EN*
*Set in IBM Aldine 12pt*
*and printed in Great Britain by*
*Billing & Sons Ltd, Guildford*

*British Library Cataloguing in Publication Data*

*Fraser, Amy Stewart*
*Roses in December.*
*I. Title*
*941.1082'092'4      CT828.F65      80-42213*

*ISBN 0-7100-0823-6*

A book goes on for such a long time;
you can read it in a few days, but
it takes years to write.

John Steinbeck

# Contents

# Acknowledgments

I offer to Colin Gibson my very warm thanks for much valuable information gained from *Highland Deerstalker* and other writings; to Diane Morgan, Editor of *Leopard Magazine* for permitting me to include 'The Dockit Hoose'; to George S. Shepherd, Editor of *The Book of the Braemar Royal Highland Society* for permission to quote from 'Men of Gairnside'; and to Peter Watson, Editor of the *Press and Journal* for permission to include 'The Lady with the Lamp at Balmoral'.

In spite of careful enquiry I have been unable to trace the owners of certain copyrights, and beg forgiveness from anyone whose rights have been overlooked.

# I
# Trivial Fond Records

Back, O Gairn, as I close my eyes
I see what was, and is, and will abide;
Still glides the stream, and shall for ever glide.
                              William Wordsworth (adapted)

Tucked away between the folds of the hills that separate the valleys of Don and Dee lies Glen Gairn, described by one far-travelled writer as 'just as bonnie a Highland glen as I have ever seen'.

The Gairn, a happy, chuckling little river, has its source on Ben A'an in the Cairngorms, and flows through the quiet glen for twenty miles till its waters join the Dee at Bridge of Gairn.

Early spellings of Gairn, which signifies 'rough water', were Garn in 1610 and Garne in 1677. The old name for Glen Gairn was Glen Gardyne; we who lived there called it simply The Glen.

Looking back to the golden days of one's youth is a gentle pastime to be recommended for solitary hours in the enforced leisure of old age. There is so much to remember – April mornings, June noons, September evenings. All golden days in retrospect, full of wonder and small surprises.

The Manse of Glen Gairn, stone-built, square and plain in the style of many Scots manses, was five miles from the nearest shops and Post Office. It had a sunny aspect and stood on a steep and winding brae overlooking the river. That rough stony brae was unsafe for cycling; only once did my mother, in a hurry, try to mount her bicycle at the front gate — she wobbled into the high wall that surrounded the garden and cut her face between the eyes on a projecting stone. Nothing daunted she returned to the house for a large handkerchief and, holding this to her face to stem the flow of blood, she set off on foot on her urgent journey to Ballater. Her business done, the doctor put some stitches in the wound, and she stepped out with the springy step of the moorland walker all the way home. The wound healed naturally but she carried a scar for the rest of her life.

The story of my childhood in the Manse has already been told at some length* but I find I have more stories to tell of that simple life that please my friends and reawaken happy memories of their own.

A candid friend likened my last book to a bottomless bran-tub from which one could fetch up an inexhaustible supply of little gifts. Here I offer my readers more Lucky Dips in the Bran-tub of a quiet life.

The farming community in the Glen was largely self-supporting. Children learned at first hand how their ancestors had lived, for the farming equipment was for the most part the same as used by their forebears, except that the horse-drawn reaping machine had replaced the sickle and the scythe. The farmers and crofters used no artificial fertilisers on their

---

*The Hills of Home, Routledge & Kegan Paul, 1973.

land, relying on farmyard manure supplemented by lime spread roughly at two tons to the acre. The horse-drawn rake and heavy stone roller were still in use and work on the farms followed the methods used throughout the centuries.

The days when a motor car was to be seen parked at every farm-house door and tractors in the yard were a long way off.

Every house had a garden in which potatoes and vegetables were grown for home consumption; there were also gooseberry bushes, red- and black-currant bushes and a few raspberry canes. In the garden, too, were usually to be found a row of bee skeps, for the Glen was ideal honey country with plentiful clover in the fields, and bounded by hills clad in rich purple heather. The traditional straw skeps were picturesque set in an old walled garden but were awkward to handle when the time came to harvest the honey and were gradually being replaced by wooden hives.

In those days one could buy a section of honey for a shilling!

The Glen now is nearly devoid of farming folk; farm houses stand empty and sheep graze where once grew oats and barley; heaps of stones and a rowan tree indicate where stood cottages we used to visit. As Betty Allan says:

> Tourist traffic's buzzin' noo
> On Shenval's steep incline
> Just passin' through
> An' very few
> Think o' the folk langsyne
> That kent Gairn
> An' worked Gairn
> An' heavy-hearted left Gairn.

The Manse, too, is a desolate ruin with birch saplings rooted among the pathetic stones. Rank grass flourishes where there was a daisied lawn, the garden is a wilderness and of the bushes of gloriously-scented roses, white, pink and yellow, there is not a trace.

I often think of Hugh MacDiarmid's lines sometimes attributed to another poet

> The Rose of all the World is not for me . . .
> I want for my part
> Only the little white rose of Scotland
> That smells sharp and sweet
> And breaks the heart.

Long ago in Scotland it was believed that a rowan tree planted near a house ensured perfect protection from evil spirits for all who dwelt there. From the humblest bothy to the laird's castle every dwelling had its guardian rowan tree. Cattle were driven by a switch cut from the tree, and a boat on the loch, like the ship at sea, had somewhere in its timbers a slip of rowan to guard it against storms and tempest.

The elder tree, too, was credited with the power of warding off evil; its old name was buttery wood because it was always grown near the dairy to keep away the Devil who might turn the butter. A more down-to-earth reason for planting it there was that flies will not go near elder.

When I was very young country couples were not married in church but in the bride's home or in the Manse, so it came about that I was present at a wedding before I could walk. The bridal couple stood facing my father in the semi-circle of the bow window. It seems that I, sidling along the carpet, elected to sit at their feet throughout the ceremony, for the bride was Annie Forbes, our young maid, with her round rosy face and beaming smile, who sometimes sang to me at bedtime her own version of 'I'm ower young tae mairry yet'. The bridegroom was Jamie Smith who some twenty years later was to be the chief piper at my own wedding.

Afterwards, the wedding party trooped off on foot to the barn at Tamnafeidh where John Coutts and his wife provided the traditional marriage feast for their ploughman Jamie and his bride who were to share her grannie's but-an-ben at the head of the brae. Meggie Maclean's thatched cottage, the last remaining of the clachan of Clashanruich, has long since disappeared, but the name lives on. On the hillside, well sheltered by trees, with a magnificent view of the valley, stands the House of Clashanruich built in 1915. The original meaning of clachan was a circle of stones, a place of heathen worship, then the word was applied to a church or chapel, and finally to a hamlet. Riach means a grey knoll, and there is a ruined chapel nearby, so possibly one may interpret Clashanruich as the clachan on the site of the chapel on the grey hillside.

I have no clear memories of my childhood before the age of three. I was often told how old James Farquharson from Balno sometimes took me by the hand and guided my earliest footsteps along the roads near the Manse, and my amused parents related how, when out walking with them, we came to a puddle and in the manner of James I raised a warning finger and spoke my first word, 'Peel'. It must have been a considerable time after that incident that I was accustomed to invade my father's study. One morning, however, I was told to run away and play, because Papa's busy. Presently a little face appeared round the door and a plaintive little voice enquired, 'Busy, Papa?' This my father could not resist; he took me on his knee and showed me pictures in his big book of exotic birds, a book that I came to know well throughout my early years.

A very early memory is of a day when having climbed on to a low chair I contrived to put my head between the horizontal bars at the back, and there I stuck. I got no sympathy from my mother who merely remarked that having got myself in a fix it was up to me to get out of it if I did not want to go about for the rest of my life with a chair hanging round my neck. Faced, as I believed, with such a horrific prospect, I twisted and turned a bit more and got free. Looking at that chair today I realise with some surprise how small I must have been – not much more than three years old, I guess. I know I had not then acquired a sister.

A grandfather clock never fails to remind me of a childhood nightmare. I was not quite four when I was taken to Montrose on a visit to friends of my parents called Dakers. A small folding bed was set up for me in a parlour in which a grandfather clock ticked away in solemn undertones, and struck the hours in deep vibrant accents. In the middle of the night I awoke feeling very frightened and alone in the strange dark room. I fumbled my way round the room, guided to a certain extent by the ticking of the clock. When at last I found the door I opened it and gazing out into the pitch darkness I wailed for my mother; I continued to wail but nobody heard me and the clock ticked eerily on. Sobbing I stumbled back to bed. In the morning I was in disgrace – my bed was wet, Mrs Dakers looked grim and my mother 'black affronted'.

From Montrose we went to Largo, the little fishing port which still smacks of the sea and ships and the ancient ways of fisher-folk. I barely remember my first sight of the statue of Robinson Crusoe in his niche above the harbour. Alexander Selkirk, the castaway sailor, was born in Largo. When bound for the South Seas he quarrelled with his ship's captain and was put ashore on the uninhabited island of Juan Fernandez. After four years and four months there he was, presumably, rescued, for he found his way back to Largo, and it was on his adventures that Daniel Defoe based his story.

My father had a great admiration for all explorers, especially for Dr Nansen, studying and following with interest his plans for the Great Polar Expedition of 1893-6. In fancy he trod every step of the way with the great man. I remember him discussing the climax with my mother, and being shown Nansen's picture, though I was only four when the expedition ended. There was an oft-told story concerning a celebration pudding which was cooked on board the *Fram*, Nansen's ship. The letters FRAM were meant to appear on it, but the pot boiled over with disastrous results — F and R came out on the famous pudding but A and M were never seen again. So ended the story of that famous 'clootie dumpling'.

When summer blazoned its pattern on the rugged face of the hills and yellow broom spilled its golden rain on the banks by the wayside, the scent of clover drifted across the Tamnafeidh fields where contented cattle grazed in the lush grass knee-deep in buttercups, or fetlock-deep in shallow water at the river's edge. There was bird song all day long from the time the sun was up until it had set; whaups too kept up one rippling call after another, sometimes through the night.

When I was very young I longed to be able to fly like the birds. Running as fast as I could with my arms flapping like wings got me nowhere, but there was a place indoors that regularly tempted me to try for real flight. Four or five steps from the foot of the stairs the hand rail stopped. I used to poise there on the curve with arms outspread and take off into space. Once I actually felt that I was flying through the air, landing as light as thistledown; I never forgot the magical moment, but though I frequently repeated the performance, landing all too heavily, I never recaptured the sensation of flying as free as a bird — it was to be nearly forty years before I flew again, in an aeroplane!

I have known Alex Duguid, who was born at Tamnafeidh, since he was a tiny boy in a minute kilt. He invariably ran to meet my mother, to carry her tin milk-pail, and escort her to the farm-house door.

He had an inborn love of flowers inherited from his mother, and learned the veterinary value of herbs from his father who was skilled in their use, making use, for example, of the little yellow tormentil (*potentilla erécta*) to doctor sick calves with gratifying success. As a schoolboy Alex wandered over the high hills as far as Ben A'an in search of the rarer Alpines, accompanied only by his treasured copy of 'Bentham and Hooker'. He sent specimens to botanists far afield and from those pen friends came plants from distant lands — Tibet, China, America — and these he grew in the garden at Tamnafeidh.

In a long life devoted to horticulture he has been writer, lecturer, consultant and judge, as well as a very practical gardener. For many years he was manager and part-owner of nurseries in Berwickshire which he developed extensively, and he has been honoured by the Royal Horticultural Society by the award of their Associate Medal for distinguished services to horticulture. His raised garden, designed for the special care of Alpines, was also hailed as a godsend to elderly and infirm garden lovers who can tend such a garden from a wheel-chair, thus bringing endless pleasure to many who had thought they would never again know the joy of pottering among their beloved plants and flowers.

My town-bred mother, on her marriage, had quickly settled down to life in the country, taking in her stride, as it were, the use of paraffin lamps and candles and the total lack of mechanical aids to housework.

I think back to the washing days of my childhood, when

the family wash was done by hand in large zinc tubs, using a ridged scrubbing board and plenty of Sunlight Soap which came in packs of two double bars and was stored till it hardened. Lines of my baby sister's long robes, flannel barracoats, and nappies of turkish towelling flapped in the breeze on stranded wire stretched between the rowan trees. The wire never rusted or sagged. I loved to help to spread sheets and pillow-cases on the drying-green to bleach in the sun. Later they were put through a wringer clamped to the kitchen table which pressed them when dry. They smelled sweet after lying out on the clean green grass.

Allan Ramsay describes the washing green of his boyhood as

A flowery howe between two verdant braes
Where lassies used to wash and bleach their claes.

and Marion Angus remembers

A bonnie drying green
Wind fae aff the braes
Liftin' and shiftin'
The clean-bleached claes.

Winds o' a' the airts
Naked wa's atween
An' heather creep creepin
Owre the bonnie dryin green.

The last time I saw the Manse drying green is was like a hay-field, and both the croquet green and the sunken garden were lost among trees that have grown up in their midst.

My mother's flat irons were used in pairs so that when one was in use the other was re-heating in front of the glowing embers of a good fire — never in front of a smoky fire which would have soiled the clean linen. When the iron was hot it was rubbed on emery paper or soap to make it glide easily,

9

and with a final rub on the ironing-board it was ready for action. As the handle got very hot a holder made of several thicknesses of material was necessary. The same applied to the handles of the cast-iron kettles and girdles that hung from a swey over the open fire. Few girls left the Glen school without making at least one kettle-holder as a Present for Mother.

My little sister, Ellie, and I loved to be out of doors in a high wind and to hear its wild cry in the tree-tops. Sycamores were the noisiest — they thrashed about and tossed their branches on the slightest pretext; oaks rode out any storm, barely moving; pines were like people swaying in the wind, their boughs moving rhythmically while their needle-like leaves emitted shrill piping sounds. To this day, I never find myself walking in pinewoods but I smell the Gairnside air, and automatically draw deep breaths.

Ellie and I would sit among the ox-eye daisies with the bank of greenery behind us, the shadow of the beech leaves making a pattern on our faces and pinafores, and the broom bushes by the drying green beyond rustling together like the swishing of silken skirts. The beeches retained their poise in a gale; they rustled graciously like a hostess in a watered silk gown, regally permitting their branches to sweep the ground as they rose and fell in a stately manner; but it was in the woods that we heard the gentle sound of the birches, James Russell Lowell's 'most ladylike of trees'.

Having learned to write I began to compose little verses and stories. I was no Daisy Ashford with her *Young Visiters**
and a friend like Barrie to write the Preface, but my father thought it was time I had something better to write on than old

---

*The Young Visiters* was first published by Chatto & Windus in 1919 when Daisy was nine. Nobody wished to correct her spelling. Her 'sublime work' was widely read and ran to thirteen impressions.

envelopes, so he folded some sheets of sermon paper, bound them together, and presented me with my first notebook.

A frequent visitor was John Reid who was born at Balno in 1838, and had been in turn farm worker, policeman-poet, and detective. I remember the genial old man who addressed me in verse as Maid of Gairn, and encouraged me to go on writing. He was a prolific writer of poetry, charming lilts in the Doric and narrative poems about historical events on Deeside, which regularly appeared in a number of periodicals.

Memories of his boyhood were woven into 'The Auld Priest's Hoose', 'The Miller O' Laggan', and 'The Kirkyaird o' Dalfad' which were published in *Modern Scottish Poets*. John never forgot the place of his birth, and paid regular visits till he was advanced in years, and continued to write long letters full of folk-lore to the Little Girl at the Manse.

In the long summer days Ellie and I never tired of playing hide and seek in the shrubbery, had our housies in the back avenue, and went visiting on the lawn which seemed to us a vast stretch of grass. For our housies we used part of a lichen-covered wall in the avenue and laid out on it our treasures — shards of brown glazed crocks lovingly polished, various curiously-shaped pieces of wood and various small white stones from the hills, with glints of quartz in them.

We marked out the rooms with ridges of pine needles, and built a tiny fireplace with cones. There we would contentedly play for hours, sweeping our floors, and preparing to receive callers. The names of our imaginary guests varied from time to time, but never our own; Ellie, as the caller, was always Lady Violet Forbes of Castle Newe, and I, the hostess, was Lady Gwendolen Hamilton of Skene. Then we reversed roles, for on these occasions we combined keeping house with our other game of Grand Ladies. We did not dare to borrow mother's flouncy lace-trimmed petticoats, nor did we do

11

more than peep at her fur stole and muff in their special mothproof box, but we did borrow sateen underskirts, straw hats and parasols, and went mincing along, daintily holding up a fold of our long skirts in the fashion of the day. From a battered metal teapot the hostess poured tea, and to a steady flow of small talk handed green-leaf plates with biscuits of daisy heads, and bits of moss off the wall for cake.

The large, rambling garden, as well as supplying us with an abundance of fruit and vegetables, was full of old-fashioned flowers — pyrethrums, monk's hood, bachelor's buttons, canterbury bells, peonies, and the glorious heavy-scented pheasant-eye narcissus.

The woods, too, were full of flowers.

There never seemed to be time enough for all the ploys we were engaged in as each new day came on the heels of the old — so much we wanted to do, so fleeting the time to do it in; so much pleasure to be taken, as it were, on the wing — that was the pattern of our childhood summer.

With its sunshine and flowers, summer was the time for picnics.

When the school skailed at three o'clock Ellie and I would hurry home hoping for a picnic at the Milton Burn. As our homeward road was by the riverside we occasionally saw a heron at the river edge, or standing motionless, deep in thought, on one leg in the water. If we inadvertently disturbed him at his fishing he would immediately take off, legs and neck stretched out and wings flapping lazily away over the fields. The little water wagtail, too, haunted the Gairn, darting from stone to stone where he balanced with his tail comically going up and down.

The word 'picnic' is a term of common speech not yet 200 years old, but the picnic itself is much older, even the Greeks had a word for it. No climate in all the wide world is less propitious for picnics than the climate of Scotland, yet we Scots continually rush out-of-doors to eat a meal on every possible occasion, and so do our fellow-Britons.

Mrs Beeton considered a well-arranged picnic one of the pleasantest forms of entertainment. The party, she advised, should be composed principally of young men and women, two or three good-natured old gentlemen, a few pleasant children, and one, only one, dear old lady to take charge of the commissariat and make sure nothing essential was left behind, such as mint sauce for the cold lamb or fresh butter for the lobster, for the Victorian picnic was remarkable for its size and solidity. Our family picnics were primitive in comparison, with lots of home-made scones and jam. Much as we loved picnics we never longed to emulate Sir Walter Scott visiting Melrose by moonlight, nor to partake of a picnic meal in the eerie haunts of the magician, Michael Scott, but we were in good company in our love of al fresco parties.

Romantic to the backbone, Queen Victoria and the Prince Consort revelled in the wild scenery and the solitude of the hills after the formality of life at Court. In her *Journal* the Queen describes expeditions to Glen Gairn, Morven, Glen Muick, and Glen Feshie as well as more distant places. On the hill-tracks they rode sturdy shelties, which also carried the food for the picnic. The state of the weather never bothered the Queen; she describes how one day they lunched on the hill looking down on Loch Muick, in a bitter wind, beside a cairn, with their guests grouped round them; and, another day, how a mist came down on Lochnagar, and they had to sit very still till it lifted, because there was a precipitous drop near by. On an average picnic, the Queen and Prince Albert sat on boulders covered with tartan plaids, and a cloth was spread at their feet by kilted attendants. They enjoyed game pie and cold roast venison, balancing their plates on their knees. On one occasion the Prince scribbled on a scrap of paper that they had lunched at that spot, placed the note in a seltzer bottle and buried it.

They were by no means the pioneers of the al fresco meal in Scotland. Banqueting in the open air is an Old Scots Custom, as we may gather from the diary of John Taylor, who attended a deer-hunt in the Forest of Mar three centuries ago. He wrote that there were many kettles and pots boiling, many spits turning and winding, and 'a great variety of cheer'.

As we grew older we were able to go farther afield, but not for us the lure of wide horizons – we were content to walk or climb. Once, when climbing Morven, we were thrilled by the sight of a majestic golden eagle slowly wheeling above the grassy slopes, its underwings showing white patches as it turned.

Years later, Dr Janet Smith, alone on the top of Morven, lunched at Lady Mary's Well, a place she dearly loved, and found a baby golden plover, one of the most beautiful chicks she had ever seen, its plumage like shining gold.

When we climbed Morven we approached by a track through the hills from the Mullach to the ruins of Morven Lodge.

Mrs Duguid of Tamnafeidh followed the same track when she used to visit her mother in Logie Coldstone, beginning her sixteen-mile journey round Maamie to Morven, stopping only for a bite and a sup with George Coutts, Charles Gordon's shepherd, who lived in a cottage on the hillside called Bothanyettie. Rested, she continued her journey round the base of Morven and over its shoulder to her destination and a warm welcome that awaited her. Next day she returned home by the same route, completing a trip of thirty-two miles, and thinking nothing of it.

This was the road my father used to take when he visited his scattered parishioners in the Braes of Cromar. In those days there was a right of way, a footpath through the hills; when I last looked for it, it had disappeared, overgrown with heather.

We took friends to the top of Lochnagar, and recalled that Byron was only fifteen when he climbed it with a gillie by way of Ballochbuie and the rocky burn called the Garbh Allt. He scrambled up unassisted, in spite of his lameness, and spent a long time on the summit, obviously deeply moved by the grandeur of the scenery.

The trees in the Forest of Ballochbuie might have been felled like those on forests lower down Deeside, and sent raft-like down the river to Aberdeen, had not Queen Victoria acquired it and saved the ancient pines.

Years before, a Macgregor sold it to a Farquharson for a tartan plaid; when the Queen bought it from Invercauld she referred to it as 'the bonniest plaid in Scotland', and had these words engraved on a cairn set on a wooded hill over-looking the Dee near Balmoral. Her way of commemorating the chief events in her lifetime, from a royal betrothal to a national victory, was to have a cairn erected on a nearby hill.

Sometimes we hired a wagonette and took our friends to the Linn of Dee or along the wild and lovely moorland road, with gorgeous stretches carpeted with crimson bell-heather, which brought us to remote Lochindorb with an island in the middle. On it, in the fourteenth century, stood a castle, fastness of the piratical son of King Robert II, the Earl of Buchan, better known as the Wolf of Badenoch, who burned down Elgin Cathedral. A wagonette was a four-wheeled horse-drawn open carriage. The driver sat on a crosswise seat high in front, his passengers sat facing inwards on a bench fixed on either side. We entered by a door at the back. There was no space allowed for luggage, so our picnic baskets, or, if we were going on holiday, our large strapped leather bags and Japanese hampers must have been accommodated under our feet.

Japanese hampers were useful pieces of luggage because they held so much. I believe their correct name was Pilgrim Baskets. They were made of closely woven Italian basket work, came in various sizes, and looked like two baby's cots when placed side by side. When one half was filled to capacity the other half was placed neatly over it and the whole unwieldy bundle was secured by a broad leather strap . . . two, if necessary.

We sometimes took friends to see the Colonel's Bed. This was a mere ledge in a rocky gorge in Glen Ey where the 'Black Colonel' of the ballads, a Farquharson of Inverey, found safe hiding from the redcoats after the Battle of Killiecrankie, in which he had fought on the side of Claverhouse. He lay there safely concealed for a considerable length of time. Food was taken to him daily under cover of darkness by his devoted sweetheart, Annie Bhan.

While in Inverey we would often have a word with Maggie Gruer, a great talker and a most hospitable soul. For fifty years she welcomed weary hill climbers, cyclists, and tourists from all over the country, and never turned one away from her cottage door. She had known John Brown, and once she skelped a dog that had been chasing her cattie, and then found that it was a royal 'dug' and belonged to the Prince of Wales. She was very fond of her cattie, 'Ramsay Macdonald', who once disappeared, and later astonished her by turning up with five kittens — she named two of them 'Morris' and 'Cowley'. She met all our reigning sovereigns from Queen Victoria to King George VI, and had danced at a Gillies Ball with King Edward VII. After her death her plain wooden, purely functional, armchair was bought by Mr Hugh Welch who presented it to the Cairngorm Club. At the Annual General Meeting of the Club the President sits in Maggie's chair. Thistle Cottage has been modernised and ought to bear a plaque stating 'Maggie Gruer lived here' – perhaps one day it will.

John Lamond was the forester's little boy at Corriemulzie near Inverey. From early childhood he was a star-gazer; perhaps the clear frosty nights so often seen in Braemar imbued in him a longing to study the stars. He was a bright boy at the village school and a wonderful opportunity came his way for satisfying his thirst for knowledge – he was offered a place in the Scots Benedictine College at Ratisbon in Bavaria, where a few promising Scots boys received free education.

There were no stage coaches from Braemar in those early days. Even the mails were brought 32 miles from the nearest post town, Kincardine O'Neil, by a postman who made the journey on foot three times a week. So Johnny Lamond, not yet twelve, on his way to begin his studies for the priesthood, had to be taken to Aberdeen on one of Donald Gruer's farm carts. We can picture them setting out on a bracing October morning in 1817, the bottom of the cart well lined with straw, Johnny sitting on a bale, his little trunk with all his belongings beside him, while Donald sat on the 'fore breast' of the cart and guided the plodding horse. They were two days on the road – two nights at wayside inns. At Aberdeen Johnny was left in the care of Father Gall Robertson from the Monastery. They embarked on a ship bound for Rotterdam, and thence sailed up the Rhine, arriving at Ratisbon on 1 November.

From that day the little lad from a remote clachan, alone

among strangers in a strange land, had no communication
with his home and family, and never returned to Deeside. He
completed his course in Philosophy, Theology and the
Classics, but when the time came for him to be ordained he
decided that it was not his vocation. He then had a brilliant
career at Munich University, became Director of the Royal
Observatory, and later became Professor of Astronomy at
Munich University. He was created a Knight of the Bavarian
Cross with the title Johann von Lamont. He died in 1879, an
astronomer with a world-wide reputation. The Deeside Field
Club erected the memorial to Johann von Lamont, Astronomer
Royal of Bavaria, which stands in his native village at Inverey
and there were Lamonds present at the unveiling.

The father of Inverey-born Margaret Rees, another John
Lamond, was taxidermist to the Royal Family, and mounted
a large number of antlers which are on show at Mar Lodge.
Margaret, on a visit to Sandringham, made a point of seeing
some of the 'Royals' which her father mounted so many years
ago and are still proudly displayed.

In Braemar stands the house which was known at one time as
'the late Miss Macgregor's cottage', but Robert Louis Stevenson
thought 'The Cottage' sufficient address. There in 1881 he
spent seven disastrous weeks of wind and rain, and occupied
the time in writing *Treasure Island* to please his stepson.

Where the road from Glen Clunie enters Braemar lie the
ruins of the eleventh century castle of Kindrochit,* once a

---

*In 1925, Boy Scouts directed by the historian, Dr Douglas Simpson,
excavated the ruins, where crumbling walls had become smothered with
rank grass and bushes. It was then that the ancient Kindrochit Brooch
was unearthed. I had an interesting correspondence with Douglas
Simpson at the time, and had his permission to make lantern-slides of
his drawings of the excavations and of the brooch.

hunting seat of King Robert I. At times a ghostly company is said to be seen seated round a table heaped with skulls and treasure. Had Louis, as his friends called him, discovered the castle and its legend, he might have woven it into another of his great tales of adventure.

Louis had gone to Braemar in search of health, and was agreeably surprised that he felt so well, in spite of 'blighting weather as cold as March'.

*Treasure Island* published as a serial aroused little interest, but when it appeared in book form it was an instant success. William Ewart Gladstone got a glimpse of it one evening in Lord Rosebery's house and spent next day hunting the London booksellers for a copy. He later declared that the tap, tap, tap of Blind Pew's stick haunted him as few things in fiction had done; and Barrie's mother, Margaret Ogilvy, said she could not sleep till she had seen Jim Hawkins safely out of that apple barrel.

In the hall of my home stands a little tub, craftsman-built from pinewood from the Forest of Birse, reminding me of my meeting with old William Brown, the only man in Scotland still engaged in the traditional country craft of bucket-making. His father and grandfather before him had owned and worked the century-old mill on the fringe of the Forest; the original timbers, small windows and lack of electricity showed how little it had changed since his father took it over in 1853. William was always busy for his bucket-making was a one-man business, and he had customers all over the world. From local timber he cut his requirements and his small kiln for drying the staves was heated by logs and sawdust. Water from the Finzean Burn supplied the power to turn the big wheel that worked the machinery — a primitive arrangement of smaller wheels and bolts. Precision and perfection were the inspiration of a craft most fascinating to watch.

With a lingering look at the old beams, the solid wooden floor, the huge water-wheel and William at work at his bench made of great slabs of granite, I turned away. The Finzean Burn chatters among the pines, the mill is derelict and William has gone, but while my little tub stands in the hall holding a favourite plant, I shall always remember the bucket-maker of Finzean.

We tramped through the woods of the Quoich on many occasions, till we came to the Earl of Mar's Punch Bowl where the eleventh earl once filled a pot-hole with punch. He and his followers then dipped their quaichs in the stone basin and drank to the success of the rising on which they were embarking. The raising of the standard on the Braes o' Mar was planned at a meeting in Glenbuchat Castle on Donside. The actual standard was not the familiar Scots banner but a very special one worked by the Countess of Mar and her ladies who sat busily embroidering day after day in the withdrawing room in the Old Castle of Mar, to have it ready in time for The Day. It was made of blue silk richly embroidered in gold, bearing on one side the Arms of Scotland and on the other the Thistle of Scotland. What a pity it no longer exists!

We* often went to picnic by the Burn of the Vat – the Vat being a large natural rocky cave where the freebooter, Gilderoy, often hid from his pursuers. His actual hide-out was in a recess behind the waterfall in the cave, the water providing a concealing curtain.

Another interesting place was the Peel Ring of Lumphanan. Some castle or fort must have existed in ancient times. It lies on the direct road over the Cairn O' Mounth and the path of the ancient highway leading from the Peel may still be traced. It was said to be the road taken by Macbeth when he was

*See *The Hills of Home*, page 216.

being chased through the woods where he later met his death in a hand-to-hand struggle with Macduff. Defying midges and what are laughingly called 'summer showers', we tended to favour lochans and out-of-the-way places for our picnics, but when we craved a breath of sea air we went to Stonehaven. No sooner had we seated ourselves on the harbour wall, with a bag of crusts, than excited herring-gulls came wheeling in on strong wings, swooping and diving and crowding round our feet, the little brown half-fledged ones cheeping protests at their elders who pushed them aside, muttering in gull language, 'You're on your own now', and snatched morsels from under their baby beaks, leaving them hardly a crumb. The noise was deafening.

Four hundred years ago the poet Dunbar would have described it

> The air was dirkit with foulis
> That cam with yammerin and youlis.

We frequently went to see Mr Mercer, working single-handed at his loom in the small woollen mill at Gairncliffe beside the river, at that point very rough water, near the Bridge of Gairn. My mother had a travelling rug woven by him. For five years it accompanied me to school in Edinburgh and kept me warm on many a cold journey in unheated trains. Still in use, with not a single broken thread in its makeup, its faded moorland colours still admired, who would not today be pleased to acquire a hand-loom woven rug of pure wool for the modest sum of fifteen shillings!

Those were the days when Alec Keiller, the young Laird of Morven, used to dash up and down the narrow roads in his new motor car, the first seen in the Glen, often with Christian Lumsden, a school-girl passenger who shared his love of speed. Once they overtook me walking on the Delnabo road

— whoosh — with a toot of the brass horn they were gone, leaving me clinging for dear life to the paling. The Lumsden family, tired of eternal winter snow on Deeside, shortly afterwards sought the sun in South Africa where Iain Wilkinson, the well known journalist, found them years later enjoying their new life.

The young Laird claimed that he could cover the distance between the new Morven Lodge and the ruins of the old one in four minutes. On one of his trial runs he took Alexander Spence, his forester, who held his breath during the terrifying mile-a-minute trip. It was no doubt a hair-raising experience, but Spence held on to his hair and his hat with both hands.

Years later Alec flew the first monoplane to be seen on Deeside and kept it in a hangar near the Bridge of Gairn. The old folk were much impressed. One old man was overheard telling a crony — 'Man, ye missed a treat! The machine wis that gracefu' . . . jist like a hen fleein'.'

Years before he became a well known archaeologist, Alec had a magnificent collection of vintage cars, all pre-1914, which Salmond, his majordomo, used to display discreetly with natural pride to his personal friends. I often wonder what happened to them. Alec retired to Wiltshire where he devoted his life to archaeology, his excavations of Roman remains being of notable importance.

Situated at the foot of Craig Leek stands the home of Captain Alwyne Farquharson, of Invercauld, M.C. Chief of Clan Farquharson. The house commands a fine view of the high peaks of Lochnagar and Ben A'an, and just beyond the pines of Invercauld, the majestic heights of Beinn-a-Bhuird.

Not far away stands Braemar Castle, built in 1628 by the Earl of Mar; later it was attacked and burned by the Black Colonel of Inverey. English soldiers were garrisoned in the restored castle when the Jacobite cause was lost at Culloden.

Within living memory, before the days of motor-buses, a horse brake ran daily between Braemar and Ballater carrying passengers, parcels, and the Royal Mail; it was owned by a contractor called John Milne. Major Milne of that family was with the 51st Division of the Gordon Highlanders in the First World War. Most of the men in D Company were from Braemar, Glen Gairn and Ballater.

John Macdonald was then the deer-stalker at Mar Lodge; his grandfather used to spend weeks alone in a bothy in the hills during the shooting season to warn climbers off the hills. The old man often spoke of two earthquakes which were felt in the neighbourhood in November 1890. That was before I was born; now I, too, can tell my great-grand-children of two earthquakes that shook Carlisle and the Borders in the winter of 1979.

# II
# A Lady Sweet and Kind

Happy are the children who have a singing mother;
the charm of her voice follows them through Life.

Colin Brown

Ellie and I were among those happy children who had a singing mother. She sang as she went about her housewifely
tasks; she sang by the peat fireside in the evening while her
busy fingers produced endless creations, useful articles in
knitting and crochet; she sang the songs my father loved to
hear, and she made all the children in the Glen sing with her,
at the successful and popular singing class which she held at
the Manse for over ten years. I remember myself at four-
and-a-bit standing on a chair for my platform, from which to
give a performance for the sole entertainment of my baby
sister in her cot; wordless and tuneless was my offering but
I la-la-laed and put so much feeling in it that the tears of
emotion ran down my cheeks.

In a year or two our favourite indoor game was to become
'Concerts', I conducting an imaginary orchestra, Ellie the
soloist, our audience a row of chairs on which reclined an

assortment of dolls and rubber toys — teddy bears and other soft toys were unknown to us, in fact the teddy bear had not then been created.

I recall my mother rehearsing a talk she was planning to give to a women's club in Ballater — more correctly, she had been invited to 'read a paper' — on famous Scotswomen who have written songs that will never be forgotten. Sixty years later, among her papers, I found the script, which reveals considerable research on the subject.

She noted that though women are popularly supposed to be unable to keep a secret, many song-writers preferred to remain anonymous. Lady Wardlaw, for example, wrote and published 'Hardyknute', and convinced ballad-lovers that the manuscript had been unearthed in a vault in Dunfermline Abbey. Not till 1755, thirty years after her death, was the truth discovered. It is believed that she also wrote the 'Ballad of Sir Patrick Spens', which we all learned at school, but that fact, too, she carefully concealed.

Jean Elliott wrote her version of 'The Flowers of the Forest' some 200 years after the tragedy of Flodden. She and her brother were riding one day near their home at Minto when their conversation turned on the desolation of the district when all the fine young bowmen, the flower of the countryside, were slain almost to a man. Young Elliott wagered his sister she could not write a ballad on the subject, and she won it in a few days. She published it anonymously and when it first appeared it passed for an old ballad.

Some time later a grand game of mystification was going on in Edinburgh, indeed all over Scotland. Sir Walter Scott was largely responsible; he, as the Great Unknown of *Waverley*, was producing in quick succession his fascinating novels, and not even his closest friends suspected he was the author.

As for the modest women-writers, one can imagine the

mental agony they endured, partly because they wanted to remain in fashionable anonymity, and partly because, in some circles, it was not considered fitting for a lady to have literary leanings.

Lady Anne Lindsay, a daughter of the Earl of Balcarres, was one of these, a lively and witty girl, the eldest of eleven children. Their mother, a strict disciplinarian, determined that none of her family should run the risk of being spoiled, did not spare the rod. She used to shut them in dark closets, and send them supperless to bed when they were naughty, which seems to have been fairly often; but not even a diet of bread and water in a dark room could curb Anne's high spirits. One day the children decided enough was enough — they would run away, but they did not get far. Robin Gray, the surly old shepherd at Balcarres, caught the runaways, and brought them back. The punishment for each one of them was tincture of rhubarb, and Anne, as the ringleader, got the biggest dose. Years later, there was an old Scots melody of which she was very fond, but the words were poor. 'And I longed', she wrote, 'to sing the air to different words, and give to its plaintive tones some little story of virtuous distress. While attempting to do this, I called to my little sister who was playing near me, "I am writing a ballad, my dear; I am oppressing my heroine with many sorrows. I have sent her Jamie to sea, made her mother fall sick, broken her father's arm, and given her auld Robin Gray for a suitor . . . I want to load her with yet another misfortune . . . help me to one, I pray". "Steal the cow", suggested Elizabeth, "so the cow was stolen and the ballad completed".'

This letter was written to Sir Walter Scott when Anne was an old lady, and first admitted that she wrote the song. As a girl of twenty-one she had overheard a group of literary gentlemen discussing it — was it, they wondered, a seventeenth-century ballad, possibly a composition of David Rizzio, or of later date? They offered a reward of twenty guineas to anyone who could authentically fix the period — Anne, secretly delighted, said not a word.

Caroline Oliphant, the Baroness Nairne, was another who went to great lengths to conceal her identity as a writer. Many of her finest songs appeared in *The Scottish Minstrelsy*, but she wrote in a disguised hand, and signed herself 'Mrs Bogan of Bogan'. When she called on her publisher she dressed in black, with a heavy veil, posing as Mrs Bogan, an elderly lady up from the country, and played the part so well that he never guessed she was really an elegant young woman who lived in Edinburgh, not a stone's throw from his office.

My own chief interest lies in the music of the Hebrides.

Frances Tolmie, the pioneer of Hebridean folk-lore and folk song, opened a wide field of interest and delight to folk-lorists and historians. She was born at the Manse near Dunvegan. As a young girl in 1860 she tramped across Skye for miles to supervise the knitting of the crofter women in remote parts of the island, accompanied often as she went along by an old woman who sang to her the old songs of Skye. These she remembered through the years she spent with intellectuals in Edinburgh, Cambridge and the Lake District, and she became a recognised authority on Hebridean folk-lore.

Ethel Bassin, in 1977, did a great service in publishing *The Old Songs of Skye* which describes the life and work of Frances Tolmie and places her unique contribution to folk song against a full historical background.

History was simply repeating itself when, in the summer of 1905, Marjory Kennedy-Fraser put to sea and made for the Isles. She knew less about the Hebrides than she did of any foreign country; she did not have the Gaelic, and the sheer physical strain of tramping the shores and moors might well have daunted a much younger woman. But nothing daunted Marjory; for twenty-five years she went again and again to the Isles, returning to Edinburgh to spend long days and nights preparing yet another volume. She collected over 400 Hebridean songs. She re-discovered songs that had been kept alive for centuries, mainly by women who sang them at their work. By spinning-wheels in humble homes, in sheilings on the hills at milking-time, and among the fisher-folk, she listened and made notes, and gave the songs back to Scotland as part of her birthright.

It was Mairi MacDonald on the island of Mull who gave Scotland her favourite carol 'Child in the Manger', which is sung at Watch-Night Services throughout the land. Mairi was the wife of a crofter, Lachlan MacInnes, and was born in Mull in 1789. She never learned to read or write but she used to croon her little songs to the island children, and at ceilidhs among her friends and neighbours who passed them on. She composed the words and the Gaelic air of the carol at the height of a religious revival which swept the Inner Hebrides during the 1820s. Services were conducted by a band of evangelists based in Tobermory. With other crofters Mull was badly affected by the Clearances of 1840-60 and one place-name reflects the horrors of those grim times. When the village of Sorn had been 'cleared' the place was renamed Glen Gorm. In the Gaelic, gorm means blue, so the blue glen is an everlasting reminder of the dreadful days when the air was filled with blue smoke rising from burning homes.

Mairi died in 1872, and two generations later, in 1959, a cairn was erected in her memory near her birthplace at Ardtun, and all who use the Iona ferry may see it. Her little Christmas hymn lives on.

Malcolm Macfarlane of Elderslie got the original Gaelic air

from an old man, a native of Mull, and made a translation of the words. It was not till the twentieth century that a later translation was made by Lachlan MacBean, a Gaelic-speaking native of Kiltarlty, who was a journalist in Fife and died in 1931. It is his words that are in general use today, that will always mean Christmas to Scots children —

> Child in the Manger, Infant of Mary,
> Outcast and stranger, Lord of all;
> Child who inherits all our transgressions,
> All our demerits on Him fall.

Margot Fonteyn, in her autobiography, relates how her Aunt Margaret was restored to health when on medical advice she was given champagne daily during her convalescence. In those days there was a widespread belief in the efficacy of champagne as a restorative. My mother's friend, Betty Ramsay-Sibbald, wife of the minister of Crathie from 1897 to 1918, was once seriously ill and her life in danger; when she was unable to take any form of nourishment her doctor recommended her to consume a bottle of champagne every day and that saved her life.

My mother treasured a fine studio portrait of Betty, who was one of the Lochnagar Beggs before her marriage; as a young woman she had been presented at Court and the portrait showed her in her Presentation gown. This, by royal command, consisted of full evening dress and a long train, with three ostrich feathers in her hair, and elbow-length white kid buttoned gloves. Her train, I remember, was edged with mink, and would have been placed over her arm as she retired from the Royal Presence. I believe she also carried a bouquet of roses. She looked very lovely in the photograph, posing in white satin at the top of a short flight of stairs, with her long train elegantly arranged on the steps. Her 'presenter' had been Mrs Yarrow, wife of a partner in the famous Clydeside ship-building firm, who also lent her the head-dress and train. The Presentation took place at one of Queen Victoria's Drawing Rooms, very formal and dignified occasions held at Buckingham Palace. Mrs Yarrow, like all older women who presented a younger, had undergone the same privileged ordeal in her day.

From faded newspaper clippings I gather that my mother had many friends in Ballater and in various Manses in the Presbytery who helped her at the bazaars she organised in aid of Church Funds. Distance prevented them giving much help prior to the event, but they and the wives of farmers in the Glen rallied round her on The Day and staffed the many stalls. I read the names of the Misses Neil, Miss Reid of The Croft, Miss Gordon of The Jungle, Mrs Birse and Susie, and many others.

Mrs Lamond always gave her expert advice on the catering side. She was the wife of the founder and proprietor of the Loirston Hotel. Herself a superb cook, she supervised every meal that was prepared in her kitchen; her waitresses were homely, friendly, and attentive; she and her husband, working closely together, from small beginnings built up the Loirston into a guest house with a splendid reputation. The intimate family atmosphere was achieved by unwearying attention to details.

The coat-of-arms of the clan and the family crest adorned their letter-heading. There was a personal welcome to every guest on arrival.

Little freckled Georgie with his boyish grin and Lamond kilt ran to and fro on errands for the guests, and for his father, who acted as courier on the excursions by horse-drawn brake for which he was famous, and he never failed to be in the hall to speed every parting guest. Three generations of Lamonds made it their life's work to attend to the individual comfort of every guest — no wonder many were happy to return year after year to that home from home, the Loirston.

My mother had some quaint turns of speech. I remember how she would cheerfully accept an invitation to a wedding or a tea-party, would agree to knit a pair of stockings for a friend, or a jersey for a small boy, adding in a matter-of-fact tone — 'If I'm spared' — a fairly common saying of her generation, inherited from her father.

Every country has its special dishes which it is proud to claim have been handed down from mother to daughter by practice and example, as well as by word of mouth, for countless generations, and have survived, mainly because they are unpretentious, wholesome and delicious. Scotland has a splendid variety of such dishes.

My mother made tasty and nourishing soups which were also, of necessity, economical. She made Hotch Potch with mutton (beef never gave it such a fine flavour) and her Scotch Broth must have equalled that served to Dr Samuel Johnson who, when he first tasted it, said he did not mind how soon he would eat it again. Cockie Leekie, my father's favourite, is the traditional chicken and leek soup served at Burns Suppers (not that my father was ever at a Burns Supper) and Sheep's Head Broth is mentioned by Sir Walter Scott in *The Antiquary*.

Redolent of its native soil, oatmeal plays an important part in Scots cookery. My mother always stuffed a fowl, before boiling, with the traditional stuffing of meal, suet, and onion. Brose and brochan, porridge and oatcakes or bannocks, are as old as the hills, and there is the haggis, favourite food of Robert Burns, who called it 'Great Chieftain of the Puddin' Race'. It occupies the place of honour at all gatherings held in his memory.

When meat was rationed in wartime we, in Glen Gairn, found savoury mealie puddings much to our liking. With these and rabbits and hares, which were un-rationed and were plentiful in the Glen, and an unending supply of home-grown potatoes, we did not lack wholesome fare.

In the days of the Auld Alliance* haggis was sent to Scots exiled in France. At one time it was believed to be of French origin, its name supposedly derived from the French 'hachis'; it is now generally admitted to stem from the old Scots expression, to hag, meaning to chop or hack, which describes exactly how a haggis is prepared.

Many countries have some form of haggis – even the Ancient Greeks had one, which is mentioned in Aristophanes – but it is oatmeal that gives the Scotch Haggis its exceptionally fine flavour.

The food value of nettles has long been known to Scots, and in these days when stringent economy must be practised it is again being recognised and is in the news. In *Rob Roy* Sir Walter Scott tells us that it was the practice to force nettles for use as early kail. He describes how Andrew Fairservice, the gardener at Loch Leven, raised nettles under glass for that purpose. The economy-minded country housewife of today picks the young nettles when they are a few inches high, wearing gloves and using a wooden spoon to avoid handling them. She boils them in a very little water, and adds to the

---

*In the Middle Ages the Scots made what came to be called the 'Auld Alliance' with France, for mutual security against aggressions of the French conquerors of England; thousands of Scots served in the armies of Joan of Arc and later. Loch Fyne, the Loch of the Vine, is said to have been given its name because of the cargoes of rare French wines which were landed there in the days of the Auld Alliance.

tender greens about a pint of hot milk and thickens it all with cornflour.

Samuel Pepys was very fond of Nettle Porridge, which was made with the leaves of young nettles, dandelions, black currant, sorrel, water cress, mint and thyme, and an onion, all finely chopped and mixed with a cupful of barley and an egg and steamed in a basin for an hour. Sounds familiar? Of course it does! It is Pepys's seventeenth-century version of the traditional Cumberland Herb Pudding eaten on Easter Day.*

During the Second World War, an Aberdeenshire family, I was told, was often fed on kail brose made more palatable by being served together with oatmeal brose. The children took alternate spoonfuls of the two and washed them down with a glass of fresh milk.

Kail is rich in iron and vitamins; a story is told of a doctor who gave up his practice in the Highlands because there were too many kail-yairds and consequently too few patients!

When the elder trees were in bloom along the banks of the Gairn we children thought them the most beautiful sight with their clusters of flowers. Gipsies used to make clothes pegs and skewers from the wood of elder trees. Long ago Glen housewives declared that summer had truly arrived when elder flowers were in bloom. For generations the flowers were used in the making of wine. It was when she was busily engaged in making this excellent wine that Mistress Jean, the 'penniless lass wi' a lang pedigree', was interrupted by an unexpected call from the Laird o' Cockpen.

There was a belief that the wine should not be made until after 'Bees Day'. That was a day when it was noticed that the elder blossom was covered in thousands of bees which clung

*See *In Memory Long*, Routledge & Kegan Paul, 1977, page 236.

to the flowers till they dropped off, apparently intoxicated. By evening the blossom had all been worked over, the bees had recovered and flown home.

Thomas Pennant, writing in 1769, said that in the Aberdeenshire Highlands, which include Glen Gairn, the birch was used in a great variety of ways — for the roofing of houses, for fuel, the bark for tanning leather, and 'quantities of excellent wine extracted from the living tree by tapping'.*

According to a cookery book of 1876, cowslip wine was one of the most enjoyable of home-made wines.

Montgomery's lines say

> Simple sweets with curious skill
> The frugal cottage dames distil
> Nor envy France the vine;
> While many a festal cup they fill
> With Britain's homely wine.

The women in the Glen in the olden days also made their own medicines. They knew that many trees and plants familiar to them had medicinal value. They made cough medicine from coltsfoot and took dandelion tea as a blood purifier. The tansy grew in great profusion near the Manse, and had a strong distinctive smell. Tansy tea was considered a fine tonic.

The Latin name for the elder tree is *sambucus*; this was probably the ingredient that gave its name to that famous green ointment of my youth, Zam Buk.

The sap of the birch was recommended for removing unsightly spots and freckles; the juice squeezed from chopped parsley was also believed to remove freckles; parsley tea was taken for indigestion. Cowslip tea was supposed to be an

*See *The Hills of Home*, page 173.

excellent cure for giddiness, and cowslip petals were dried to make a comforting drink to cure insomnia.

Sage was commonly used for teeth before the invention of tooth-powder and even later. An old-fashioned nanny who came with the Crewdson grandchildren to Gairnshiel in the shooting season, used to make her young charges rub their teeth with fresh sage leaves, saying, 'Tooth-powder is to clean your teeth, but sage makes them beautiful.'

My mouth waters occasionally for an Abernethy biscuit such as my mother issued, one at a time, to Ellie and me with a mug of milk at bedtime. They were plain and wholesome and were almost the only biscuits we ever saw. We may have had a 'ginger snap' sometimes but we had no fancy or choco-late biscuits. Abernethy biscuits in those days were much larger and flavoursome than today's biscuits of the same name. They came closely packed, unwrapped, in a large, deep, square tin and *never a broken one among them* till they were grasped in our eager fingers.

Parlies (Parliament Cakes) were biscuits with a history. They were my father's boyhood treat in the Mearns and got their name by being favoured by Members of the Scots Parliament during its long sittings. They were made from a gingerbread mixture of flour, butter, and black treacle, rolled out like biscuits and baked in a slow oven.

Dr Samuel Johnson, in one of his sweeping statements, once declared that no woman could write a cookery book. He was wrong, of course; there was a spate of them towards the end of the eighteenth century, and it would seem that they have been producing them at frequent intervals ever since.

In Edinburgh alone, there was Mrs Glasse, who published her *Art of Cookery* in 1747; Mrs Cleland's *New and Easy Method of Cookery* was produced in 1759 for the benefit of the girls at her school; then came Mrs MacIvor who brought out, in 1773, *The Art of Cookery* as she herself practised it.

Mrs Frazer was another Edinburgh lady who, in 1791, published *The Practice of Cookery*. These famous women, whose works are prized and often quoted, were followed in the nineteenth century by the equally famous Mrs Dods and Mrs Dalgairn, and others less well-known.

In this century we have, among a host of others, Scotland's favourite, the versatile Elizabeth Craig; Lady Clark of Tilly-pronie, near Tarland, on Deeside, who published her own cookery book in 1909; F. Marian McNeill with *The Scots Kitchen* in 1929; Theodora Fitzgibbons's *A Taste of Scotland* which contains some nostalgic Donside recipes and pictures familiar to me; and Janet Murray's *Fine Feeling for Food*.

Conan Doyle in his *Duet with an Occasional Chorus* observes that 'Mrs. Beeton has been the guide, philosopher and friend of countless happy homes for more than a century'. In my mother's well-worn 'Mrs Beeton' the advertisements inside the hard covers include one for Lemco, from which one could prepare a beefy drink; Brunswick Black for stoves (sixpence a bottle); Silversmith's Soap, for cleaning silver (sixpence a tablet); Dessicated soups to add to stews, and Cakeoma, a cake mix, surely two of the earliest convenience foods! There is a picture of a massive cast-iron range, with two huge ovens with heavy doors, 'as used in Queen Alexandra's Technical School at Sandringham', and a Queen's Pudding Basin, with a metal cover which fitted over and round it, keeping water out while the pudding steamed. My mother had one of those; puddings turned out in perfect shape. Copper-bottomed saucepans are advertised for 2/9d and a vacuum cleaner for three guineas.

A typical recipe from the collection is for roast hare:

Choose a young hare which may be known by its smooth sharp claws, and the narrow cleft in the lip. It should be hung for eight days; it must then be skinned, stuffed and the body sewn up with a needle and strong cotton before trussing. Roast for two hours and serve on a hot dish with the head and ears in place.

My mother's method of cooking a hare was simple and appetising with no off-putting head and ears brought to the table.

In 1913, Dr Kenneth Fraser, my brother-in-law, author of *A Doctor Remembers*, was a very young Medical Officer in Carlisle. His landlady's chef d'oeuvre was baked rabbit which she served whole in a crouching position on a dish, its sightless eye-sockets turned reproachfully on the hapless doctor who had to attack it with carving knife and fork.

We always had plenty of eggs at the Manse so my mother never had to test the recipe which advised that two tablespoonfuls of new-fallen snow would serve instead of an egg for pancakes.

There is also in the book a marvellous dish called London Syllabub which requires a *pint* of sherry sweetened and spiced; the cook must then put into it *from the cow* about two quarts of milk. I cannot believe that even the most affluent of Londoners kept a handy cow in the back-garden for the convenience of the chef!

I have my mother's copy of that Victorian treasure *Enquire Within upon Everything*, published in 1892, the year when I was born. It not only advises on the making of a Will, the arrangements for a funeral, and other serious matters, but it gives glimpses of the domestic problems of the day, which are no longer with us – for example, we do not have to make a messy varnish for our grates, nor do we have to change the water in which leeches are kept. It also makes the astonishing claim of knowing a reliable method of Washing Kid Gloves.

# III
# The Kirk and the Castle

Come all to church, good people . . .
A. E. R. Housman

Sweet briar, honeysuckle and clematis have all been called eglantine, but most people favour sweet briar under its own name, scented as it is in wood, leaf and flower. I remember how I loved it when a child; it gave off a delicious perfume, almost overpowering after rain. There was a bush at the kirk gate and many a time we crushed a leaf between our fingers just to savour its sweetness. Recently, in an old Bible, between the pages, yellowed with age, I found a few leaves that still gave off a faint scent. The women-folk in the Glen, I recall, used to pick a sprig before entering church; a still older custom was to carry a Sabbath posy of sweet-smelling herbs and flowers such as appleringie, tansy, and the buds of the unforgettable, old-fashioned Scotch rose. Appleringie was carried into the kirk between the pages of many a Bible; it was reckoned to keep folk awake however long and dreich the sermon. Bergamot (bee balm), too, would fill the air with fragrance; its leaves used to be called 'Bible leaf', being nice to sniff delicately in church. Whatever the custom in an austere age when vases of flowers in the kirk were as yet unknown, it was a true instinct, for the Bible is all for fragrance whenever possible, and many are its references to sweet scents.

No unnecessary work was done in the Glen on the Sabbath Day within living memory. Whistling was only permitted if it was a psalm tune. My father used to tell a story about a stranger who was watching Feugh salmon leap one Sunday, when a particularly fine fish made a spectacular leap. The man gave an involuntary whistle of admiration and a policeman standing on the bridge beside him sternly admonished him, 'Ye maunna whustle on the Sawbath.'

Long ago there was an order in Scotland that no man should fish on Sunday. The order was obeyed till one Sunday Tweed salmon-fishers noticed that fish were abundant in the river. After much consultation, they took out their boats and nets and caught 500 salmon; but for over nine weeks from that day not a single salmon was seen in the Tweed.

Queen Victoria once went with her ladies for a picnic on Sunday, and afterwards heard that she had offended Crathie folk who saw it as a flagrant breaking of the Sabbath Day. The Queen, much troubled, told Dr Norman Macleod, the eminent divine, of the incident, when he came to preach in Crathie Church and was her guest at Balmoral. He in turn told her about an English visitor who had greatly displeased his host, a Highland laird, by going for a stroll on Sunday. The guest protested, 'But our Lord walked with his disciples through the fields on the Sabbath.' 'Mebbe so,' said the Highlander, 'but if they had daured to try that here they wadna hae been allood.'

The eventful Original Secession took place in 1733 when a number of ministers and congregations left the Established

Church after a succession of protests from the General
Assembly against the Patronage and Toleration Acts had been
disregarded in London. From Norah Howie I learned that her
husband's father, before his death in 1902, had been a pre-
centor for many years in the Original Secession Church in
Glasgow. Tunes such as 'Coleshill', 'Ballerma', and 'Belmont'
were used for favourite psalms but there was an aversion to
using the actual words of a psalm when practising a tune on
weekdays, so secular words were used. The Glasgow Orpheus
Choir frequently included in their concert programme a
rendering of 'Mice and Men' which was an example of the
kind of secular words sung at Choir Practice in the Original
Secession days. From an old programme I have copied the
words

> There was an auld Seceder cat,
> An' it was unco gray,
> It brought a moose intae the kirk
> Upon the Sabbath day.
>
> They took it tae the Session
> Wha it rebuked sair
> An' made it promise faithfully
> Tae dae the same nae mair.
>
> An' noo on Sabbath day it sits
> Like some auld clockin' hen,
> An' canna understan' ava,
> The weys o' mice an' men.

When practices were held away from kirk premises solem-
nity might be relaxed and children would be delighted when
their father sang

A weaver said unto his son
The day that he was born,
Blessings on your curly pow,
Ye'll gather pirns the morn.

(The rhyme actually goes back to the bad old days when tiny children were sent into factories to pick up broken threads at the weaver's loom.)

The ordination of a minister to a charge in the Church of Scotland is a solemn occasion. I have read of an ordination that took place in the parish of Auchterhouse in December, 1702, when the kirk was a primitive building with rushes strewn on the earthen floor, and the lighting was provided by home-made candles. After the service there was a congregational banquet at a total cost of £2 4s 10d. On the following Sunday the new minister the Rev. Patrick Johnson, preached; the offertory amounted to 1s — the beadle got 2d and the rest went to the poor of the parish. Conditions had considerably improved by the time my father graduated Bachelor of Divinity at St Andrew's University 189 years later, and was ordained to the Quoad Sacra parish of Glen Gairn in July 1891, at the age of twenty-eight. There had been thirty-seven candidates for the vacant charge; five preached before the congregation, and my father was chosen from a short leet of three. Depopulation had already begun but there were still 1,454 souls in the parish, 75 on the Communion Roll, and 8 elders in the church. After the long-drawn-out Ordination Service the traditional full-scale dinner took place in the Invercauld Hotel in Ballater attended by the eight elders and by various ministers representing the Presbytery of Kincardine-o-Neil.

On the first Sunday after his ordination my father noted in his new Log Book that there was a congregation of fifty-eight

42

adults and children; the offertory amounted to 3s 7½d, to which he personally added another shilling. He also recorded Sunday School classes, a Young Men's Evening Class, a Choir Practice of seventeen members, and Evening Service in the kirk. The latter was discontinued in the winter of 1893.

Before his first Communion Service, which took place soon after his ordination, he prepared twelve Young Communicants and held a Service of Preparation, known as the Fast Day. He engaged a woman to give the kirk a thorough cleaning, for which she was paid 4s, and the man who undertook to scythe the long grass which had grown up round the kirk was pleased to take it away for hay. At the first meeting of the Kirk Session my father agreed to act as Clerk and noted that the Roll now had eighty-eight members.

Tokens* were then in use in hundreds of kirks all over Scotland. They were a solemn reminder of Covenanting days when freedom of worship was not an accepted part of the Scots way of life. Covenanters were men of strong convictions who in 1638 banded together to sign a covenant pledging themselves to defend, by every means in their power, their beliefs and practices. Tokens were issued only to those who had been prepared for the Sacrament, and in those far-off days, apart from ensuring that they were held only by genuine communicants, they were a safeguard against the intrusion of Government spies during that period in history when religious persecution was rife. The kirk door was well guarded during the service and none but token-holders were admitted.

In 1894, Edwin Arnold wrote of tramping by brig and birk and cairn, looking down on Glenmuick and 'Wild Glen Gairn', and visiting Crathie Kirk, when he and his friends expressed

*See *The Hills of Home*, page 145.

surprise at the humble appearance of the church where Queen Victoria worshipped; it was an unpretentious building with whitewashed walls and a small belfry. From the earliest days of the Queen's widowhood, the people of Crathie waited outside the church door till the whisper went round, 'She's comin'.' They then went inside; only tourists remained to see her arrive, and so it is to the present day. Queen Victoria was always accompanied by one of her ladies-in-waiting, and usually some of her grandchildren. She arrived in her carriage, drawn by two of the Windsor Greys, just as the church bell began to ring, and went up to the gallery where her pew was on the left of the pulpit. The service was conducted in the usual way, and when, before the benediction, the elders carried round the old wooden ladles for the offertory, the Queen put in her offering with the rest.

Though it grieved Crathie people that their old kirk had to be laid low, they came to realise that it would rise again in a form more worthy and more beautiful.

My father was like the Clerk of Oxenforde in that 'wide was his parish and houses far asunder'. With part of his parish in Crathie he naturally was present at the laying of the foundation stone of the new kirk by the Queen in 1893, when she spoke so clearly that every word was distinctly heard by the whole assembly (and there were no microphones in those days). In the following year a Grand Bazaar was held in Crathie to swell the fund for the building of the new kirk. I possess a unique souvenir of that event, a handsomely-bound book (weighing five pounds!) called *Under Lochnagar*, a valued gift from Isabella Mackenzie, whose father was born and brought up in Glen Gairn. It must have been an immense task, undertaken with boundless enthusiasm by its compiler, Mr Profeit, with the active support of the Queen and her daughters. It contains numerous literary contributions and engravings, including a dedicatory hymn, the words by the Marquis of Lorne, the Queen's son-in-law, the tune composed by Professor Frank Bridge, who was then the organist at Westminster Abbey. It also contains a poem signed by Rudyard Kipling, and an autographed drawing by Gustave Doré. The full-page advertisements are in themselves artistic engravings. Crathie Kirk today, in its beautiful setting among the hills, is unique within the Church of Scotland. In all ways but one it is an ordinary country congregation within the national church. Its uniqueness is its connection with the Royal Family. Since 1848, when Queen Victoria first visited Deeside, every sovereign, with their families and households, has worshipped along with the local congregation Sunday by Sunday while the Court is in residence at Balmoral.

The minister of the united parish of Glenmuick, Tullich and Glen Gairn was then Rev. James Middleton, who had succeeded his father in the charge. He was not physically strong, but it was hoped that he would be able to travel between the Manse of Glenmuick and the church which had been erected in Ballater in 1801, by the pony and trap provided. He did not, however, occupy the Manse, but decided to live in Ballater village with his wife and daughter in a pleasant villa, Heatherbank, just off the Braemar Road.

Helen, a delicate, dainty little girl, was given her name at the request of the Duchess of Albany, who was the Princess of Walbeck when she married Queen Victoria's youngest son, the late Prince Leopold. She was then living at Birkhall. The little church in Glen Gairn, which I still think of as my father's kirk, nestles at the foot of a steep hill up which the road winds mile after lonely mile, past Glenfenzie, across the Glas-choille to the lands of Don and Spey.

James Grant was a crofter at Glenfenzie who later farmed at Abergairn. In an age when it was the ambition of every

Catholic family to have a son a priest, James sent all three of his sons, Colin, John and Charles to Blairs College to train for the priesthood. Colin became a famous cleric and rose to be the Catholic Bishop of Aberdeen. John and Charles did not, after all, enter the priesthood. Charles was a surgeon in the Army during the Crimean War.

John, in 1850, was a teacher in Braemar, and while there he collected material for *Legends of the Braes o' Mar* which he published anonymously in 1861. The second edition, which bore his name, was published in 1876, and in the introduction he protested indignantly that a lady who in 1868 published *The Braemar Highlands, their Tales, Traditions and History*, had plundered wholesale from his *Legends*.

Built in 1800 to seat a hundred, the little church, like so many old Scots kirks, has windows on one side only, and at the west end, where the bell hangs in its bell-cote with the rope hanging down on the outside. In its east gable is a blocked-up window which was believed to date back to the days when this was sometimes done to avoid the payment of window tax, but Doctor Cuthbert Graham the well-known authority on such matters, has pointed out that at the time the kirk was built the window tax was no longer operative and the blind window is possibly an odd architectural custom of the period.

For many years it has been my earnest hope that it will be discovered that this is one of Telford's churches as in many ways it resembles those known to have been designed by him. At present no clue to the identity of the architect has been found.

Well known for his work on roads and bridges, Thomas Telford is also remembered in Scotland for his kirks. In the years between 1824 and 1834 he was called upon to furnish plans and to arrange contracts for the erection of a number of Highland kirks and manses to be built by a Special Commission set up by Parliament in 1824. There are forty-two parishes listed in Sir Alexander Gibbs's book *The Story of Thomas Telford*. A bridge designed by Telford spanned the Dee at Ballater in 1809. It was destroyed in the Great Flood of 1829; the present bridge dates from 1885. On the South Road, not far from the bridge, is a little stream known as Spinning Jenny's Burn. From time immemorial the figure of an old witch used to be seen sitting spinning beside the burn. When road-widening altered the course of the burn she was reported to have moved higher up into the hills where she has been seen in recent years still spinning beside the stream. I should like to find out if Telford was in Ballater at the end of the eighteenth century contemplating a design for a stone bridge of five arches to span the Dee, and if he was then commissioned to design the simple little kirk in Glen Gairn which was eventually built in 1800, and his bridge in 1809.

In grievously de-populated Glen Gairn there are now few local worshippers. There is no resident minister, for the Manse was demolished many years ago. The kirk is closed during the winter months, but every Sunday afternoon in summer it is packed with worshippers from near and far. Cars are parked in the grounds, the neighbouring car-park is also full, and the 'Kirk Bus' brings from Ballater those who have no private means of transport.

The odd custom of offering pan drops ('for the sermon') at the door is observed (with a warning to the children not to crunch), and a warm personal welcome extended to all on stepping inside.

There are bunches of country flowers on every window-sill.

The minister, the Rev. James Blyth, welcomes the congregation to the peace and beauty of the Glen, with a cordial invitation to join in the worship of God with thankful hearts, and the hearty singing of psalms and hymns is uplifting and heart-warming.

The ancient pewter goblets and salvers are in use on the Communion Table, but tokens are no longer distributed, and the old offertory ladle was discarded a long time ago.

The kirk door remains unlocked throughout the week and hundreds of tourists visit the church and sign the Visitors' Book. Page after page shows that a large number of the signatories are from overseas — Canada and the United States, Australia and New Zealand, Norway and Sweden, Holland, Denmark and Italy are all among them. From time to time, in August and September, the signatures include those of the Queen and members of the Royal Family and their guests, who stroll along from Dalphuil, the Old School House, which for nearly forty years has been a royal picnic cottage.

Over a cup of tea the other day a friend and I were recalling some of the hymns which in childhood days in Sunday School we loved to sing such as 'Gentle Jesus, meek and mild' and 'We are but little children weak'. Before we had enjoyed a second cup we had made quite a verbal list of old favourites now seldom heard. We recalled 'Tell me the old old story', 'Safe in the arms of Jesus' and 'Do no sinful action' which Kenneth MacKellar recorded so beautifully in Paisley Abbey.

We sang together, my friend and I, a few lines from 'The fields are all white' and 'What can little hands do'; there we sat, two very 'Old Girls' indeed, remembering over the teacups what good tunes these old hymns had, and humming, between mouthfuls of cake, snatches of 'Shall we gather at the river'.

Today new hymns, often bearing the stamp of folk and pop music, are riding in on the winds of change, and young voices praise the Lord in a new idiom. Rock, jazz, western and calypso tunes have appeared, and modern hymns set to pop music are sung in many Youth Clubs.

Sidney Carter's popular 'Lord of the Dance' was adapted from a Shakar tune, and has gained enough impetus to be included in 'Hymns for Today'. It is, as we all know, a 'grand tune for singing', but I confess I have never become reconciled to hearing the words

> . . . and they hanged me high
> and left me there on the Cross to die

sung in that rollicking manner.

My father always wore clerical garb, wearing out his old black trousers when working in the garden (his black silk topper in its leather hat box was kept for special occasions like weddings and the General Assembly).

Annie MacHardy, a round, rosy, middle-aged housekeeper undertook the steady job of starching and producing a high gloss on his clerical collars and cuffs. The cuffs opened out flat for ironing and were closed by cuff-links in wear. She also laundered his clerical bands — two pieces of fine lawn joined at the top and tied round the neck, worn under the chin and lying flat on the velvet yoke of his heavy ribbed silk pulpit gown. His hood was lavender silk lined with white satin and edged with white fur — the Bachelor of Divinity hood of St Andrew's University.

He carried to church a clean copy of his sermon notes written in his clear hand on orthodox sermon paper, the pages stitched together so that there was no fear of notes fluttering from the pulpit. He never omitted to pray for the reigning sovereign, for the Royal Family and for those in charge of the affairs of the nation.

On his annual visit to Edinburgh for the General Assembly of ministers of the Church of Scotland he spent all his free hours on the Mound and the Bridges wandering from one old bookshop to another completely absorbed in reading, lost to all sense of time and place. When he returned home at the end of Assembly Week his worn leather portmanteau was heavy with books and a fresh supply of sermon paper. He had a well stocked library of the classics, biographies and books of travel, mostly acquired at second hand.

June, the month of roses, has long been a favourite time for weddings. It is remarkable that comparatively few hymns are listed as being appropriate for singing during the celebration of a marriage. Years ago 'The Voice that breathed o'er Eden' held first place. It was written, at a friend's request, by John Keble.

Henry Francis Lyte's version of the 103rd psalm 'Praise my soul, the King of Heaven' was first broadcast at the wedding of Prince George, the Duke of Kent, and Princess Marina and has been much in favour ever since. Brides today tend to choose hymns which are dear and familiar at all seasons such as 'The Lord's my Shepherd' and 'Now thank we all our God', but probably the hymn written by Dorothy Frances Gurney for the marriage of her sister continues to be first favourite.

'We were all singing hymns round the piano one Sunday evening', she told a friend, 'and my sister, turning to me said, "What's the use of having a sister who writes poetry if she can't write new words to my favourite tune!" I replied, "Well, if nobody disturbs me I'll go into the library and see what I can do." In a short time I came back with "O Perfect Love" and she was delighted. I have always felt that God helped me to write it.'

Mrs Gurney was also the author of the much-quoted lines —

> The kiss of the sun for pardon
> The song of the birds for mirth
> One is nearer God's heart in a garden
> Than anywhere else on earth.

My husband and I were the first couple to be married in the church in Glen Gairn; since then a great many brides and their grooms have elected to come from a distance to make their vows within the quiet sanctuary with nothing but the song of the birds to break the encompassing silence.

In 1918 my Father received a call to the parish of Southwick, on the Solway coast, in the Presbytery of Dumfries; so it was Goodbye to the Glen where he had ministered for twenty-seven years, to begin a new life in very different surroundings where most of his parishioners owned large dairy farms and their wives engaged in the making of Dunlop cheese.

There were a number of ministers from other parishes in the Presbytery at the Induction, who were afterwards entertained by Charlie McKerrow and his wife at Boreland of Southwick.

My mother invited all the wives of the ministers to tea at the Manse. She herself had arrived only the previous day. She who all her life had declared to unexpected visitors, 'You must take us as you find us', hospitable as ever, presided with dignity and composure at this her first meeting with her new friends, and begged them to 'make themselves at home' and enjoy the good Scotch tea she had prepared. Later, the ministers called to collect their wives, and a very informal atmosphere was at once created.

In years to come my father often exchanged pulpits with

one or another co-presbyter, a special friend being the Rev. Douglas Cochrane, the minister from the neighbouring parish of Kirkbean which now, with the parishes of Colvend and Southwick, forms one united parish under one minister, who occupies the Manse of Colvend.

Down on the rich merse lands near Carsethorn is the estate of Arbigland. When Colonel and Mrs Blackett resided there hares were preserved as well as game birds. None of their tenants were allowed to possess a shotgun or to own a dog, but in spite of these restrictions they were good kind landlords. The Colonel was keen on keeping fit and loved to take exercise; sometimes when being driven home he would get out of the dog-cart and run behind it.

Admiral John Paul Jones, the founder of the American Navy, was a Kirkbean lad, his father being Head Gardener to the Craiks of Arbigland; Dr James Craik of Arbigland was a friend of George Washington, and Surgeon-General Cavens was the negotiator of the subsequent Peace Treaty. It is remarkable that three men from the same little-known parish should play such important roles in that historic war, and, therefore, not surprising that numbers of American tourists should find their way to quiet rural Kirkbean.

I am indebted to Mrs Lorna Lyon of Port Ling for lending me the charming book *In Unity*, written by her kinswoman, Janie McKerrow, in which she reveals a way of life in the Southwick of long ago. From this book I learned that women in Southwick had always been accustomed to work in the fields, and, in fact, in early times when the men, of necessity, had to go off hunting, the women tilled the fields and planted the crops. There was regular employment for both men and women on the farms. In potato seed-time the women arrived early carrying milking stools, and sat in a semi-circle round a cart-load of potatoes which had been couped in the yard.

Each woman, armed with a small potato-knife, soon cut up the load of potatoes, preparing them for planting, leaving one or two 'eyes' on each piece. Their wages were small — within living memory two shillings and threepence a day was the general rule, and half-a-crown or three shillings a week for doing milking — yet all were warmly clad and well fed, mainly on oatmeal, garden produce and eggs from their own hens.

During work on the farm they got buttermilk and potatoes in abundance; they had tea once a day with plenty of cheese and occasionally meat. Rabbits and burn trout made a pleasant change, what they called 'a nice dinner'. The March Fair and the Dalbeattie Show were their only outings.

All the cottage folk, like the crofters in Glen Gairn, had chaff beds. On threshing day the women would arrive with two sacks apiece, each carrying a riddle to sift the chaff. It took two sacks full of sieved chaff to fill a mattress. Surplus chaff was not wasted; some of it was put in the farmyard midden to absorb some of the liquid manure.

Martinmas was the most important day for farm workers in most districts of Scotland. It was at the Hiring Fair that they were given the opportunity of staying on at their farm or of seeking employment in another 'place'. For many it was their first and only holiday. They had money in their pockets to spend on Jews harps, pocket knives and other ferlies. Shopkeepers were on the look-out for careful lads with hard-earned cash to spend on clothing and boots.

I remember seeing the tall, heavy metal milk containers, known as churns, at wayside collecting points in Southwick. At one time, in some districts, the number of churns on their platforms at lorry-level was a certain status symbol. As one passed along a main road one noted the single churn of the small farm and at another spot the six or seven of the larger dairy farm.

The disappearance of the milk churns is a small but significant change in the countryside. The collection of churns ceased many years ago. Milk is now collected direct from the farm by milk tankers from refrigerated vats. The churns were not churns as we had previously known them; they were tall galvanised vats, holding ten gallons of milk, heavy but convenient receptacles for the lorry-man to man-handle from their wayside platform on to the lorry.

In 1940, Southwick farmers were asked to leave their heavy machine tractors out in the fields; this was supposed to stop the possible landing of enemy planes!

My father ministered in Southwick for fifteen years till his retirement in 1933, having completed forty-two years in the ministry. He calculated that he had preached nearly 3,000 sermons, and occupied a hundred different pulpits, many of them on repeated occasions, in parishes all over Scotland and on the English Border, as well as in hospitals and prisons, and on board the S/Y *Meteor* and the S/Y *The Midnight Sun*.

In the year 1977 some of my family and I were happy to meet Mrs Gemmel Gourlay, the artist who now resides in the old Manse of Southwick. She received us with great kindness and hospitality and showed us round her beautiful modernised home, which was a nostalgic experience for me.

Canvases were stacked in what was once my father's study with its window facing towards the church he loved so much. In the kitchen my thoughts kept turning to the old cast-iron range, and the paraffin lamps that had to be filled and trimmed daily in the 1900s. My thoughts kept turning to my mother preparing the seating arrangements in the morning room for a meeting of the Women's Guild; I could see her stacking card tables for a whist-drive in the school in aid of the Soup Kitchen, or getting ready to preside at the monthly meeting of the 'Rural', for she took a keen interest in all parish activities.

Mrs Gourlay showed us how she had converted the coach-house into an attractive studio and then my young folk told her they used to have races round the garden, and held Mini Sports Days in the paddock, with Woolworth's shiny metal egg-cups as Presentation Cups for the winners.

# IV
# Travellers All

The sheep with their little lambs
Passed me by on the road.
Katharine Tynan Hinkson

Before the Scottish and English railways amalgamated in
1923, of the five independent railway companies in Scotland
the Great North of Scotland Railway, although the smallest
of the lot, was the only one to use the term Great in its title.
But that was typical of the GNSR through its whole life – a
proud and independent railway if there ever was one. But no
longer does a shrill whistle call our attention to the cream
and brown coaches of a Great North of Scotland train pulling
out of Ballater, nor a plume of steam trace the route of the
line to Aberdeen. On 28 February 1966, amid scenes of
mingled excitement and regret, Ballater Railway Station was
closed. Many words were printed about this much-publicised
small station which unrolled its red carpet to six generations
of royalty, offering a genuine welcome to them and their
famous guests, as well as to countless hordes of 'visitors'
(never called tourists) who thronged its single platform,

returning year after year when it was fashionable to take a house in Ballater for The Season.

No writer, however, on that occasion recalled that at Cambus o' May, a short distance along the line, a tiny station, already closed, stood high in a birch grove so close to the river that, according to McConnachie, 'you might almost fish from the carriage-window'. Nearby still stands the cottage that came to be known as the Dockit Hoose, with an interesting history, linked with the Great Floods, the Muckle Spate of 1829. It was built on the site of an old Ferry Inn, which was not a public house in the modern sense of the word, but was established as a spital, or temporary place of rest for shepherds and drovers taking their flocks and herds by slow stages to sell at one of the trysts, making their way by the steep Cairn o' Mounth. (Cambus o' May, by the way, should be Cambus o' Maigh, for Cambus means a bend and Maigh a flat place; there is an acute bend in the river there, and the land on both sides is flat.) Many a weary mile the drovers 'traivelled' – maybe a couple of months on the road, from the time the cattle or sheep were collected till they were finally sold at one or other of the big markets that disappeared more than a century ago. The autumn tryst at Crieff was important in the seventeenth century, but in the latter part of the eighteenth century it was shifted to Falkirk to meet the convenience of the increasing number of English drovers who came north to attend them. The drovers slept among their cattle on the journey south, and sometimes accompanied the beasts, when English dealers had bought them, down to the pasturages of south-west England for the final stages of fattening.

There is an old right-of-way by the Lairig Ghru Pass from Rothiemurchus to Braemar. Cattle and sheep were driven over it to a sale held every year at Braemar, and there was much crossing of the Lairig. The young girls of Rothie-murchus used to travel through the pass in groups of four or five, each carrying a basket of eggs on her head to sell in Braemar. Nowadays it is mostly hill-climbers and hikers who use the pass. The Spittal of Glen Shee (a corruption of hospital or hospice) appears in ancient records as a great gathering place during the days of droving. A spital was usually a well-built stone house with a dry floor, a thatched roof, and rough-and-ready accommodation. Dog-tired men were thankful for small mercies, even a shake-down in the loft. Wrapped in their plaids they were snug enough. The Ferry Inn, however, was badly situated and when the river was in flood it inevitably suffered. During the Moray Floods of 1829 the rivers and burns of the north-east of Scotland rose to unprecedented levels and caused severe damage and loss of livestock. In that Muckle Spate the occupants of the Ferry Inn had to flee for their lives in the middle of the night, as related by Sir Thomas Dick Lauder. He published a book on the Moray Floods, of which he had been an eye-witness from his home at Relugas. 'The deluge of rain', he wrote, 'fell chiefly in the Monadh-Leadh Mountains and in the Cairngorms. It came down so thick that the very air itself seemed to be descending in one mass of water upon the earth.' Among the rivers affected were the Spey, Don, Dee and Gairn. Sir Thomas described a journey he made down Deeside some time later:

I stopped at a little inn called Cambus o' May, kept by a respectable couple Mr. James Ogg and his wife. The bank here is eight or ten feet high, and Mr. Ogg's home stands on it on a level haugh, having little more than the breadth of the road between it and the stream. The river burst its banks suddenly on the morning of 4th August, the second day of the flood, surrounding the house and rose five feet in it. The Oggs, wading up to their waists, were glad to escape to the hillside, without having time to remove anything to the upper storey. They returned next day to find the house half-filled with mud and sand. They had lost three ankers of whisky and one of rum, as well as furniture, carts, and corn. 'Saxty pun' wadna cover oor loss', lamented Mr. Ogg. 'An' fat think ye, sir', exclaimed Mrs. Ogg, 'the verra first thing I fand fan we cam' back wis a bit trootie i' the plate-rack, soomin' aboot amang the dishes!'

'A trootie in the plate-rack!' said I, 'that was something! Did you fry it?' 'Na, na', said Mr. Ogg, 'she couldna fin it in her heart tae hairm it fan it had cam', as it were, tae oor verra hearth-stane for shelter, sae I pit it back i' the river an' it soomed awa!'

In a field near the Ferry Inn flints were found some years ago, and experts were then of the opinion that, as there are no natural flint rocks in the district, this must have been the work-place of men who collected them elsewhere and fashioned flint implements in prehistoric times. There are Pictish remains in a neighbouring wood.

The turnpike road constructed in 1855 left the old road and passed on the right of the Ferry Inn, and between house and river there remains a stretch of the old highway. The railway which, in September 1853, had been inaugurated between Aberdeen and Banchory, was extended to Ballater in October 1866. Plans had been published in 1864 of 'The Proposed Railway from the Charlestown of Aboyne to the Castleton of Braemar'. These were subsequently modified to include a line, for goods only, from Ballater to Braemar. The embankment was actually built to a point just beyond the Gairn but no farther. (The bridge which was to have carried the line over the Gairn now carries the road over the Gairn at Daldownie.)

The Railway Company took over the land on which the Ferry Inn stood, and made some essential improvements, including a slated roof, for thatch would have been a hazard when sparks were flying. As the house stood so close to the planned track, it was found necessary to slice off a piece of the gable-end to let the trains go by; thus it became known as the 'Dockit Hoose'.

In 1952 the Rev. William Sawers, Minister of Dinnet, wrote:

When the Company acquired the land the house was improved to some extent. The clay floor was covered with wood, but as there is no air-space under it the floors and walls have always been damp. No effort was made to install an indoor water-supply, or even to provide outdoor sanitation. When the corner of the house was cut off, indoors the original stonework was still visible while the rest of the room was wood-lined. The house is still liable to flood when the river is high; the present tenant often has to carry furniture upstairs, and on one occasion at least, within living memory, the occupants have had to be rescued from an upper window. When the pump freezes there is a scarcity of drinking-water, and they have to cross the highway and carry water from an overflow from the pond at the Hotel.

For many years the Dockit Hoose stood empty; now it has been re-named and modernised and is once more happily occupied.

Not only did the cattle-drovers travel great distances from the north to the sales – they came also from the south.

Elizabeth Dodd recently described the Falkirk Tryst in her grandfather's day: how he travelled from Penrith in Cumbria to Falkirk to buy sheep, and how he, with the help of hired drovers, brought them south by easy stages. The flocks were gathered on Stenhousemuir where each owner paid for a stance and did his best to keep his own flock in its allotted space – no easy task, for the sheep had probably never before been away from the peace and security of their native hills. The noise of the fairground, where upwards of 20,000 sheep were gathered, where strange men stood and stared, where strange dogs ran about in a most disturbing fashion, was very unsettling. The noise of bleating sheep, barking dogs and shouting men mingled with the sound of much haggling and bargaining.

Wandering over the Muir were alert men ready to assist buyers who were unable to do their own reckoning. At last the bargains were struck, the sheep bought and paid for; then came the job of obtaining help to get them on their way. When hiring drovers, those with a dog received sixpence a day more than the others.

Elizabeth concludes:

In 1858 Grandfather had bought 1800 sheep, and it was no easy task to gather them from different parts of the fairground to give each man his drove of 200 sheep, and set out for home. Once clear of the Fair, the sheep were laid up for a night's rest before setting out in earnest for the South. The routine walk was about eleven miles a day – three days travelling and one to rest. The nights were spent on the hills, or on private ground, where payment had to be made. The men spent the nights in any handy shelter, a shepherd's hut, a barn, or out in the open; always two men kept vigil over the sheep while the others slept, walking round the flock all the time to see that none strayed. Every morning the sheep were counted, to every man his drove, then on their way again. The counting was done by the old Celtic method —

> Yan tan tethera methera pimp;
> Sethera lethera hovera dovera dick;
> Yanadick tanadick tetheradick metheradick bumfit;
> Yanabumfit, tanabumfit, tetherabumfit
>     metherambumfit giggot.

Grandfather counted aloud, and a man stood by his side with a stick in which he made a notch every time Grandfather said Giggot.

From early April to early May there is little sleep for shepherds. April is the usual lambing month in Glen Gairn, and it sometimes brings a belated blast of Arctic weather — 'the teuchat's storm', they call it, because peeweets return to their nesting-places about that time.

If snow comes, with gales to pile up the drifts, farmers have a desperate time working under severe conditions to save their sheep and lambs. Somebody must always work the night shift, for a lamb will freeze to death on the ground if it is not on its legs within half an hour of its birth. For many years David Fraser of Balno spent long nights alone in a bothy at Ardoch at lambing time, keeping his ewes under constant observation. Weakly lambs in a flock, born in the snow, are brought indoors and kept warm, sometimes in front of the kitchen fire. Motherless lambs must be bottle-fed and then found foster-mothers.

It was Chae Downie, I think, who once told me that long ago the shepherds on the Sandringham Estate lived in a caravan during the anxious weeks of lambing. It was a great relief to all concerned when the last lamb arrived safely and the shepherds could return home to wash and shave, which traditionally the men did not do during the lambing season owing to some age-old superstition. From May to July the lambs are watched and cherished, their good points noted both for showing purposes and for selling, at the big sales.

Apart from one or two small farms, most of the acreage of Glen Gairn now consists of hill-pasture for the hardy Black Face sheep, those little sheep of the hills and the glens established in Scotland for over 200 years, and very much at home among boulders and heather. Their wool is coarse and well suited to the making of rugs and carpets. Some of it is exported to Italy as filling for mattresses. Owing to its springy texture it is much in demand. Scoured fleeces may be seen displayed in the windows of department stores in Naples and other towns. An Italian girl will buy raw wool for her bottom drawer, being careful that there is no colour in it. They have a superstition that black fibres, or even grey ones, might lower the state of her fertility as a bride.

In Cyprus, the filling of the bridal mattress is accompanied by elaborate ritual; the wool is first blessed by the priest, then the married women dance round it and after laying it out in long strands they place these in the form of a cross. Finally, before the cover is sewn on aromatic herbs are scattered over the wool.

Farmers in Glen Gairn always had grazing rights on the hills adjoining their land, and the arable land was worked on the traditional rotation of oats, turnips, hay, oats and three years in grass.

In the old days shepherds went south with their employer's

flocks before the winter, returning in spring for the lambing. Small farmers could not afford to do this so the winter care of sheep was often associated with rescue work in blizzards.

According to my young cousin, Paul Watchhorn, whose life is devoted to the breeding and care of sheep, it is in the Border counties that the most celebrated flocks of Cheviots have their folds.

Sheep shearing, known as The Clipping, is one of the busiest seasons in the sheep farmer's year. A sheep is not clipped till it is sixteen months old; after that the fleece comes off every July.

Fifty years ago or more, it was the practice in some parts of the country to immerse sheep in a stream to get rid of impurities before clipping. It is now far less common, largely because the higher price paid for washed wool is to a great extent offset by loss in weight. Sheep-washing among the Cheviots takes place about a week before the clipping. The Black Faces escape this indignity for as their wool is sold 'on the grease' it is said to keep better and the grease is turned into lanolin.

In all weathers the hardy intelligent collies kept by all sheep farmers are worth their weight in gold to the shepherds of the hills and may be seen pricking up their ears in eager anticipation of the round-up, known as the Gathering of the sheep off the hills in preparation for the clipping.

The hands of George and Norma Mackie, after a strenuous day at the clipping, are beautifully clean and soft, due to the amount of grease in the large number of fleeces they have handled during the day. On many occasions I have watched this husband and wife team at work, he working rapidly and neatly through the shearing of his flock, handling the electric clippers with care so that the surface was left in even ridges and not a blemish on the skin; she deftly rolling the fleece as soon as it came off the sheep's back. Wool rolling is an art in itself, the fleece of a Cheviot being rolled with the wool inside, and that of a Black Face with the wool facing outward. Norma rolled each fleece expertly and speedily into a neat bundle which she placed at once in a sack, and as the day wore on, more and more sacks were filled. Not a scrap of wool was wasted. Loose tufts were picked off the ground and placed in a separate sack and at the end of the day the place was left tidy, showing not a trace of the extensive operation.

I was reminded that a hundred years ago children collected the wisps of wool left by sheep on fences and blackthorn barricades where wool got entangled. They took them home to their grannies who spun the wool and made little blankets of it.

There is an old song which was a great favourite of Sir Walter Scott. Its opening lines are 'Tarry oo, Tarry oo, O tarry oo is ill to spin', meaning tarry wool is difficult to spin. It goes on 'Card it weel ere ye begin'. It refers to the old custom in the hilly districts of Scotland of smearing the wool of the Black Face sheep with a mixture of tar and grease to protect it from the wet and cold of winter. When clipping time came round the grease had been absorbed and the tarry part had come away from the skin but was stuck fast in the wool which it had matted together. The tar had to be removed by oil and scouring, and the wool patiently teased out by hand before it was ready for spinning.

The noise of 1,000 sheep and perhaps 1,500 lambs cannot be described in mere words; it must be heard to be believed, and after clipping it goes on for hours. One would think that every ewe had a different bleat and every lamb a different cry, since after their temporary separation mothers and their offspring eventually find each other, and at last there is blessed peace.

65

Sheep sales are held from July to early September. Four-year-old sheep are sold off as 'cast ewes', and the less good ram lambs go with them to local sales; the pick of the flock are taken to bigger sales in the south.

The restless nature of Herdwick sheep, and the manner in which they are prone to leap over boundaries on the Cumbrian Fells, gives point to the saying of the description of a persistent delinquent, 'He breaks bands like a Herdwick tup'. It was the task of restoring these sheep to their rightful owners that gave rise to the periodical 'Shepherds' Meets' at many places in the Lake District. Seton Gordon often spoke of the wild sheep he encountered at the head of Glen Eanaich, where the summer sheilings used to be, far below Brae Riach in the Cairngorms. They were originally domesticated but a few ewes with their lambs had been missed when the gathering took place. The flock increased when some of the lambs grew to be rams and carried on the race. Their wool was long and ragged, and they were very wild, scampering away at the sight of him. He thought it remarkable that they survived in the corries throughout the long winters when snow covers the high ground for months at a time.

On the shores of Loch Kinord on Deeside graze the Black Sheep of Dinnet, a strain of the Welsh Mountain Sheep. Only at lambing time do they see grass and they stay on it till they are clipped then back they go to Morven for eleven months. They are not susceptible to diseases when kept in such natural wild conditions.

I have also seen the Earl of Mansfield's flock of Jacob's Sheep which live in the park at Scone Palace. In the Palace hangs a picture painted in India in the early eighteenth century. The painting is of a ram of this most remarkable breed, indicating its origin from the Far East, legendarily descended from the flock that Jacob acquired from his

father-in-law. Their wool is greatly valued because it is very
thick and soft.

During the lovely summer days not long ago when the very
hot weather kept us, like Jane Austen, 'in a continual state of
inelegance', I sat out-of-doors every day, lifting my eyes
from my book from time to time to watch the stream of cars
that slides rapidly by on a road where once only an occasional
farm-cart rumbled along on wooden wheels. Coaches and
caravans pass every day, but the old horse-drawn gipsy
caravans are no longer seen in these parts.

Fifty years ago we in our brand-new Morris Cowley overtook one lumbering along a narrow winding road near
Stonehaven, and a cheery gipsy woman, travelling at its tail,
looked over her shoulder and called to assure us, 'Jis' wait til'
we get tae a wee wide bit o' the road, an' we'll let ye bye.'

I know nothing of gipsies today, nor how far they have
adapted their traditional ways to modern living; years ago I
made a close study of their history, their clans, and their
customs. I possess a faded booklet, published in 1876, which
tells the history of the Faas who were the gipsies' Royal
Family. It is dedicated to Esther Faa Blyth, who was at that
time the Gipsy Queen. When she first had a visit from George
Borrow she was reluctant to talk until it became apparent
that her visitor knew much of the Romany language. Only
then did she speak freely. Borrow was the first of many to go
and live among the gipsies, to learn their customs and their
language.

Sir Walter Scott borrowed many original characters to
figure in his novels, and Keats felt sure that Meg Merrilees,
who was Jean Gordon in real life, had been among the
gipsies who frequented caves along the Solway Coast. Jean
Gordon was born at Kirk Yetholm in 1670. She married

Geordie Faa and had nine sons who were all jailed for thiev-
ing. Geordie was killed in a brawl, and Jean, when an old
woman, was ducked in the River Eden at Carlisle after
shouting abuse at the townsfolk for sticking the heads of
rebel soldiers on iron railings in Rickergate.

Horn spoons in my possession were made by the Ayrshire
Kennedys — their staple industry for generations. They were
in the habit of paying for the privilege of camping on a
farmer's land, or for sheltering in his barn, by making spoons
for him and his family. The small ones were called cutties and
were intended for the use of the children. They were made
by softening a ram's horn in hot water, and moulding it in
the hands.

Gipsies are quick-witted as a rule, and Jenny Kennedy was
no exception. When she called at a farmhouse door one busy
morning, the good-wife was not inclined to listen to her list
of wants. Jenny tried to wheedle something out of her by
using flattery — 'a fine big handsome wumman like you!' —
to which the busy wife retorted wearily, 'I'm sorry I can't
return the compliment.' Quick as a flash came Jenny's reply
— 'Na, but ye cud hae telt a lee — same as I did!'

Romany people do not like to be called gipsies — just
travellers — and they dislike being confused with tramps who
were originally workers in tin, making and mending pots and
pans, from which is derived the name variously given them of
tinkers, tinklers, or just tinks. Many tinker men in the past
were skilled pipers, with a rare knowledge of old bagpipe
tunes. They would take up a stance wherever they thought
they could attract an audience. I remember seeing one years
ago playing to a small group of sightseers at the Falls of
Leny, near Callender.

A tinker couple who roamed the Angus by-ways many
years ago went by the name of Pints and Sweet Marie. They

sold bootlaces, hence the word pints, a local term for leather laces derived from the metal twist of fine wire which made a lacing point for the bootlaces.

The Capel Mounth, the ancient track that crosses the Grampians from Glen Clova to Glen Muick and Deeside, was a tinkers' road long before it became popular with hill-walkers.

For years the Scottish Development Department urged on Local Authorities a sympathetic attitude to travelling people, especially over winter quarters. The Secretary of State, acting on the recommendation of a thorough report on such people, authorised a 75 per cent grant to all Local Authorities which provide caravan sites or private accommodation. The conditions in which some travelling people have chosen, or been forced, to live have long caused concern. Their children are expected to attend school, but as they are constantly on the move, it has been difficult to enforce regulations. Many children have had the scantiest of schooling. There is growing appreciation, especially among younger parents, of the importance of education — their elders were never very interested in acquiring it. They got along with the minimum — enough to enable them to carry on such activities as horse-dealing at the annual Trysts.

They fit with difficulty into modern urban society; that is why in some areas there have been bitter clashes between them and the authorities, several of whom refused to implement the Act requiring them to provide sites or houses for families. Some families do not want to be housed; they have a saying, 'The house is good for the house-dweller', but they are not house-dwellers; others, tired of constant harrying, may try to settle down in one place. How long the travelling people will find it possible to make a living and to survive the hazards of modern road conditions, is anyone's guess. They are subject to harassment because they camp where they have no legal rights. The first need, then, is for sufficient *suitable* camp-sites to enable them to keep within the law, but it will be a long time before the majority fail to respond to the Call of the Open Road.

Drovers travelled because it was their job; gipsies liked to be known as travellers or the travelling people, because of their inner urge to move on and keep moving; many well-known people liked travelling on foot for its own sake.

In her charming autobiography, *Memories and Gardens*, Marion Howard Spring tells how she and her husband loved to walk everywhere. They had no car nor wished to own one. On one occasion, when they walked from their Cornish cottage to call on their artist friend, Lamorna Birch, their intention was to walk back, but he insisted on sending them on their homeward way by car. 'It was so difficult', she sighs, 'to make people believe that we *liked* walking!'

George Borrow was a great walker. Once, he tells us, he walked 112 miles from Norwich to London in 27 hours, at a cost of 5½ pence for a pint of ale, a half-pint of milk, two apples and a roll of bread.

William Hazlitt wrote that 'one of the pleasantest things in the world is going on a journey, but I like to go by myself. I see no wit in walking and talking at the same time. I like solitude for the sake of solitude!'

The Wordsworths were keen on walking; Charles Dickens thought nothing of a round of five-and-twenty miles; Thomas Carlyle liked walking in silence, with no interruption to his train of thought by any companion. There were some prodigious walkers among the Haldanes of Cloan. One who had been ill was welcomed back to the kirk by the minister with the kindest of enquiries. The future Lord Chancellor suggested they might take a stroll next day as he felt equal to a little exercise. In the morning they set off; in the evening they returned, the minister completely exhausted, the other apparently as fresh as when they set out.

Two hundred years ago the Barclays of Ury were famous for their strength and endurance. One of them, the Member of Parliament for Kincardine, was the first of a noted trio. At the start of each Parliamentary session, he made his way to Westminster on foot from his home at Ury, a distance of 500 miles. His son (the one who could lift a horse) also walked to London from Ury in ten days. Captain Robert Barclay, the third of that line, became known as the athletic wonder of his day, and certainly Scotland's greatest walker.

William Ewart Gladstone was still a great walker when past middle age. When he was Minister in Attendance at Balmoral he went for a daily walk of three hours' duration, and was very pleased when he walked a measured mile by the side of the Dee in twelve minutes.

A hundred years have passed since Robert Louis Stevenson gave immortality to a donkey. His belief was that if you go on a walking tour you must go alone, in which he agreed with Hazlitt, but not with Borrow who was always on the look-out for human contact and conversation. Louis, as a boy, went for solitary walks in Wick, and on one of his holidays in France with his mother spent most of his time tramping through the countryside. 'You shouldn't have had a tramp for a son,' he jokingly told her. Thomas Stevenson, Louis's father, found respite from business worries in daily walks, which sometimes carried him deep into the country with some congenial friend, and sometimes kept him wandering in the town from one old bookshop to another (like my father in General Assembly Week) and scraping acquaintance with every dog he met.

Andrew Forsyth spent several days in Glen Gairn, on foot with a camera, capturing on film places in Glen history as recorded in *The Hills of Home*, and the woods surrounding the ruins of the Manse. A dedicated photographer and a perfectionist, he makes of every subject a beautiful picture.

Anna Smith, in her entertaining memories of *My Deeside Days*, recalls the long country miles she covered as a child from a little wayside station, on her way to Findrack and its red-roofed smiddy, the farm where the railway ran through the fields. She, a nine-year-old 'townie', renewed her delights in blaeberry time, in visits to the old lady who tied balls of wool on long strings to the mantelpiece for her numerous kittens to play with, in being allowed to ca' the huge bellows on what appeared to be an 'oot fire', and watching the embers glow again. She enjoyed gathering sticks and fetching water from the well, roaming the moors with the country bairns, and exploring byres and barns. All her life she has been a tireless walker, and today in her retirement we find her still stepping out briskly on long country walks.

When the Earl of Dalhousie, whose name is perpetuated in the ancient bagpipe tune 'Fox Maule', wished to mark the occasion of a royal visit to Glen Mark in 1861, it was to Robert Dinnie, father of Donald, the famous athlete of Victorian days, that he entrusted the building of the canopy of the Queen's Well, a spring of clear water in the heart of the glen.

Once known as the White Well it was renamed after Queen Victoria and Prince Albert stopped there and found the clear cold water very refreshing. They had journeyed from Balmoral by way of Glen Tanar, Mount Keen, and a track called The Ladder. Partly as a memorial to the Prince Consort, who died not long after, Fox Maule had the water sheltered by that imposing crown of granite which rises to a height of twenty feet and is surmounted by a cross. The spring bubbles up into a circular stone basin bearing in raised letters the words

> Rest, traveller, on this lonely green,
> And drink and pray for Scotland's Queen.

In Glen Esk Folk Museum I have seen a very attractive model of the Queen's Well.

Birkhall is a white harled house in a secluded garden close by the meeting of the waters of Muick and Dee. It was built in 1715 by the Gordons of Abergeldie and about 150 years later it was sold to the Prince Consort, who intended it to be a Scottish residence for the Prince of Wales. Edward sold it to his mother in 1885, and it has been part of the Balmoral estate ever since. Queen Victoria from time to time lent the house to various members of her Court, including Sir James Clark. My cousin, Professor Kenneth Lowe, is, like Sir James, a Royal Physician and Member of the Royal Household.

In my childhood it was Sir Dighton Probyn, Keeper of Her Majesty's Privy Purse, who occupied Birkhall. Now it is the Queen Mother's summer retreat, and has been enlarged, beautified and completely transformed. Prince Charles has a favourite pool in the Muick near by, which he has fished regularly since he was a little boy with his first rod.

Birkhall has seen many famous visitors but few have made a more imperishable mark on history than Florence Nightingale, who well over a century ago stayed there for a short time. Sir James Clark wrote from Osborne inviting her to stay at Birkhall, which was at that time his summer home. She was weak and ill and he felt that Highland air would do her good; besides the Queen had expressed a wish to meet her and to hear at first hand of her experiences in the Crimea.

Florence determined to use the opportunity to convince the Queen of the need of immediate action in Army reform.

She armed herself with facts and figures, and tried to have the answer to every question the Queen might possibly ask her. She intended to ask for a Royal Commission to enquire into conditions in barracks and military hospitals, and she knew that Lord Panmure, the Minister of War, would shortly be in attendance at Balmoral. She worked day and night to get her case prepared, and on 19 September left Edinburgh with her father for Birkhall. Two days later she was commanded to appear at Balmoral for an afternoon's talk with the Queen and the Prince Consort. 'She put before us', wrote the Prince in his diary that evening, 'all the defects of our present military hospital system and the reforms that are needed. She is extremely modest. We are much pleased with her.'

'I wish we had her at the War Office,' wrote the Queen to the Commander-in-chief. Florence was invited to Balmoral again and again. She went with the royal party to church, dined informally with the Queen and Prince, and at the Gillies' Ball was seated with the Royal Family. The Queen often paid private visits to Birkhall, arriving alone and unannounced, in her little pony carriage, going for walks in the woods, between showers, with Florence, and staying to tea.

Wearied by the endless conferences, Florence's father departed; Birkhall was chilly, it rained incessantly, he caught a cold, so he went home. Florence stayed on. She charmed Lord Panmure, who agreed to the appointment of a Royal Commission, and promised to let her see the plans for a new hospital at Netley. Conversations, he said, would be resumed when they were both back in London. So when she left Birkhall the prospect was rosy. For the first time in history the living conditions of the private soldier, his diet, his treatment in sickness and in health, would be investigated.

So she passed on her way — the chronic invalid who lived to a great age, who came down in history as The Lady with the Lamp, and badgered the great ones in the land until she got what she wanted.

Another famous guest was invited by Queen Victoria to go deer-stalking with a Balmoral gillie. The writer, Janet Graham, describes how he crouched beside a rocky outcrop among the heather surveying the landscape with a benign gaze. The mountain air was pungent with peat, and a light mist drifted across the glen. Down in a corrie stood the stag that he and the gillie had been stalking for five hours, a splendid five-pointer. The stalker whispered 'There ye are, sir, . . . the Royal down there . . . get him while ye can.' Slowly the novice raised his rifle, squinted along the sights and paused; then, to the stalker's amazement, he laid down the rifle, pulled out a sketch-book and pencil, and spent precious minutes drawing the proud beast in loving detail. 'Och, the man's daft,' groaned the stalker to his fellow-gillies that evening, 'He missed the chance o' a lifetime for a wee bit picter.'

The sensitive animal lover was the artist, Edwin Landseer, and his wee bit picter became one of the most popular of British paintings of all time — the magnificent 'Monarch of the Glen'.

Queen Victoria had at various times Indian Rajahs as her guests at Balmoral. Every one of them travelled with such a retinue of servants and relations that these usually occupied most of the rooms in the Fife Arms Hotel in Braemar. The dark men with their colourful garments and turbans were a source of wonder to us and all the local children.

Dame Nellie Melba and Madame Adelina Patti were two

notable singers who were among the guests at Balmoral. Madame Patti used to go up to Braemar on the Sunday of her weekend visit to join in the services at Saint Andrew's chapel.

# V
# New Roads and Old

Does the road wind uphill all the way?
Yes, to the very end.

Christina Rossetti

At the beginning of last century there were as yet few
carriages in use on country roads; in fact, there appears to
have been very little travelling by wheeled vehicles in
Scotland. The Wordsworths, in their carefully kept diary,
state that they met only one stage-coach during their tour in
1803 and that one was on the road near Lockerbie.

It was a steep, rough, winding road that Queen Victoria
and Prince Albert travelled when they first 'discovered'
Balmoral. The greatest hazard on that road between
Blairgowrie and Braemar used to be the Devil's Elbow;
generations of motorists had to use all their skill in negotiat-
ing it (passengers in horse-drawn vehicles had to climb slowly
on foot). Now the notorious Elbow has been by-passed by a
fine new road that has ironed out the difficulties experienced
on the old hairpin bend.

The Cairnwell Pass is the highest road in Britain and has

for centuries been considered one of the most important Scottish mounth tracks and is very old indeed. It is thought that when Malcolm Canmore was King of Scotland in the eleventh century, he and his retinue journeyed north on it to the royal hunting seat of Kindrochit Castle in Mar.

The pass was used for hundreds of years by the farming fraternity of Upper Deeside who took their sheep and cattle by it to the fairs held at Perth and Stirling. The first carriage road engineered through the pass was not built till the second half of the eighteenth century; before that it was a very rough sheep and cattle track.

When we Frasers made our infrequent trips over the Cairnwell Pass in the 1920s in our first small car, a snub-nosed Morris Cowley of a bilious shade of green, known affectionately, for some forgotten reason as Imshi, we made a habit of resting briefly at the base of the hairpin bend, where there was a stony little mountain stream. This rest was intended to allow 'Imshi' to cool down and to give her a drink from the stream. We then looked round for a sizeable stone, took a deep breath, and began the climb, I seated next to the driver with my heart in my mouth and the sizeable stone in my lap, the theory that should the car stall on the hill in mid-climb I would jump out and place the stone under a rear wheel. Mercifully, the theory was never put to the test — 'Imshi' climbed slowly and steadily and never boiled.

As we came over the hill from Braemar we were reminded that Gairnside was once a country of upland farms as can still be seen from the patches of green and the number of larachs among the heather. Another new road is envisaged, nearer home this time, actually in Glen Gairn. When the time is propitious it is understood it will branch off the Ballater to Gairnshiel road at a spot near my cottage where a pure, sparkling stream comes tumbling down the hillside from its source on Geallaig.

When, fifty years ago, we rebuilt the old cottage, with its walls over three feet thick, we had the old-style open fire-place reconstructed so that we could enjoy a blazing fire of pine-logs and peats from the moss near Glenfenzie, which, to my husband was one of the chief delights of a holiday in the Glen. Now heather has grown over the moss roads. No one cuts peats any more; more convenient sources of heat are now available. The new road will, I hope, bypass the old lime kiln beside the burn, then cross the fields, and the 'rough water' of Gairn, and wend its way over the farmlands of Tamnafeidh, An Torran and Shenval to join the road to Tomintoul.

After the Jacobite Rising of 1745, bridges were built to link up the roads that were necessary for the movement of troops. The road-making was done by the military, but the bridge-building was entrusted to local men. The bridge at the Spittal of Glen Shee was built in 1749 and the builder is believed to have been James Robertson of Dunkeld. It still carries all traffic over the Cairnwell.

Fraser's Brig in Glen Clunie, built in 1750, carries traffic to Braemar by the old road. No one can now tell who Fraser was; he may have been the master mason in charge of the Clunie men engaged in the building of the brig, or he may have been the same Alexander Fraser of Durris who built the Bridge of Dye. Then there was the Invercauld Brig whose graceful arches have stood since 1752, and the Gairnshiel Brig, built in 1751, having given unbroken service for 230 years, deserves to be gently treated and eased into purely local traffic when the long-awaited New Road comes into being. No longer then will coaches have to crawl over the brig, with the passengers following on foot; no longer will motorists have to face the Shenval Brae (once a Test Road in the days of Motor Trials) which climbs to 1,738 feet over the Glaschoille before dropping down into Corgarff. The hump-backed bridges were so designed to help high water to flow through when the rivers were in flood. The road over Fraser's Brig used to enter Braemar by the left bank of the Clunie; it now passes down the right bank by way of Auchallater. The old road is sometimes used on the day of the Braemar Gathering to take the pressure off the newer road.

The ruined sheep-fold at the foot of the Shenval Brae is probably an ancient rede, a link with the past when flocks and herds had to be guarded overnight from attacks from prowling wolves. Redes may be seen in various places but that particular one is significant because it was at Shenval that the last wolf seen in the Glen was killed.

Adjoining land belonged to the Macgregors of Dalfad. The most important Macgregors in the north were concentrated in Glen Gairn, at Inverenzie, Rhinochat and Recharcharie.* Dalfad was the Laird's house, on the site of which was built the Manse sometime before my father's ordination as parish minister. Dalfad was the rallying point of the Macgregors, their assembly point being the long haugh down beside the Gairn. All were prominent in both Jacobite Risings. Twenty-four of them marched away to Culloden and eighteen fell on that fatal field.

Long ago the main road through the Glen was narrow and steep beginning its twisted course at the top of the Culreoch Brae. There, at a bend in the road, a semi-circular projecting lay-by had at some period been constructed to allow for the turning round of the carriage and pair of a somewhat morose elderly lady who made that spot the extent of her daily drive.

*See *In Memory Long*, pages 32-3.

Now the road is wide, its bumps have been ironed out, it winds less, and Black Netty's Corner has long disappeared.

Across the water at Inverenzie lived Lewis McKenzie, with whom I went to school. Even as a small boy he showed the ingenious disposition which was to prove itself in later years. He loved inventing things. Once he invented a cannon, using part of an old drain-pipe. Unfortunately, it exploded, demolishing some outbuildings, for which ploy he was soundly 'skelpit' by his irate father.

When he was fifteen the farm was given up, and the family moved south. As a young man Lewis became a protégé of the Empress Eugenie, then living in retirement in Chislehurst, and received much encouragement to develop his innate love of engineering. On the outbreak of war in 1914 he joined the Naval Brigade and drove an armoured car, but, after being badly gassed, he was withdrawn from the front line. His expertise in engineering being recognised, he was employed on the development and maintenance of the Rolls-Royce engines and the Bentley Rotary engines of primitive wartime aircraft. It was on Bentley cars that he was to achieve international fame between the wars and after.

Within the cult of vintage cars Lewis was known everywhere as 'Bentley Mac', and in all literature pertaining to the movement he was known as 'The High Priest'. In the 1930s he built and raced his own Bentley, the now famous 'Bluebird'. His son Lewis recalls the thrill of being a passenger in 'Bluebird' at Brooklands and other circuits. Passengers were permitted in those days, and indeed in some types of cars were a necessity, manipulating fuel pumps, etc.

Lewis had now become a celebrity in the racing world, and received many Honorary Fellowships. When he ceased to race himself he acted as the Official Scrutineer for the RAC at race meetings up and down the country particularly at

Silverstone. The racing tradition was carried on by his son Donald.

Bentley Mac died in 1956, and at his funeral, which was intended to be private, there was an unexpected cortege of over twenty vintage Bentleys. Bentley enthusiasts everywhere decided that the High Priest should have a memorial. This took the form, not of a statue or monument, as was first suggested. A Scrutineering Bay was erected to his memory at Silverstone. It is known as the McKenzie Memorial, and the plaque was unveiled in 1957 by his wife Mary (his boyhood sweetheart from Ballater, whom he married in 1920) in the presence of a large gathering.

His son Lewis, who had intended to become a rubber planter in Malaysia, volunteered instead for the RAF. All through the war years he flew Lancasters in Bomber Command, which were generally acknowledged to be the finest bombers of the Second World War. There was no second pilot on a Lancaster – everything depended on the skill of one man. Lewis subsequently joined British Airways, and for twenty-eight years was a pilot on all the long-distance world routes – a wonderful and very happy career.

A hundred years ago the lonely traveller on the Lecht Road between Corgarff and Tomintoul could see the rotting survivors of a number of eight-foot posts, which had long ago been erected to show the line of the road when it was deeply covered with snow. It is believed they had been put in position after the tragedy of The Lass o' the Lecht.*

Travellers about to begin the climb of the Lecht road at Cock Bridge notice, away on their left, on a height, Corgarff Castle which was built in 1597 as a hunting seat by the earl of Mar, and figured as a rendezvous when the first Jacobite

*See *The Hills of Home*, page 30.

Rising was being planned in 1715. A little army was encamped there for some days, and then marched to Braemar where the standard of King James was raised.

Thirty years later the Castle again played its role. The Jacobites, however, were forced to leave in a hurry, and Government troops destroyed the magazine, hurling the powder, musket balls and firelocks into the Don and the Cock Burn. After the collapse of the Rising the Government used the Castle as a base for hunting down outlaws and rebels. A similar garrison was established at Braemar Castle.

Corgarff Castle is the centre of the ballad *Edom o' Gordon* which relates that it was the scene of a terrible outrage in November 1571. In the absence of the Laird, his wife, Margaret Forbes, was burned to death with her children and servants, 27 persons in all, by a party of Gordons who beseiged the Castle and burned it to the ground. This was the first of two fires which destroyed the Castle. It stood derelict for many years and has now been restored as it was prior to 1748, the whole enclosed by a loopholed curtain-wall.

# VI
# Mists and Mellow Fruitfulness

Autumn nodding o'er the yellow plain . . . .
James Thomson

With the passing of summer my parents reluctantly turned their thoughts to the cold months ahead and the urgent need to replenish their winter stock of fuel. The saw-horse was brought out of its dark corner in the barn and my father and mother together worked the two-handled cross-cut saw, cutting up logs to stack in a handy pile for future use. The sawdust that accumulated in the process was scattered over the coal that was heaped in another corner and sawdust and coal would eventually burn together.

There were autumn gales when we would be awakened by the rattle of windows, the blatter of sleet on the slated roof of the Manse, and a sough of the trees in the avenue.* After such a gale there were pine roots on the hillside to be salvaged; my father wrenched them out, split them, and dragged them downhill to be dismembered for winter firing. His peat-barrow

*See *The Hills of Home*, page 60.

84

was necessary for the transport of the roots which made superb kindling, their fibres heavy with resin.

There was nothing so cheering in the chilly days of late autumn as to be greeted by a wood fire which cast dancing shadows round a room; or later, to come in, rosy from a snowball fight, to the warmth and comfort of the living-room where a crackling log-fire welcomed us. Some woods, of course, made a better fire than others. Birch was our main source, being plentiful in nearby woods; logs of applewood scented a room; beech logs burned bright and clear; oak logs made grand burning, but fir was inclined to give off sparks and had to be carefully guarded.

On our earlier picnic outings we often filled baskets with fir cones we picked up under the trees and these made a gladdening blaze on a dull day. My mother would often throw a handful on a stubborn fire and soon there would be a bright revival, and a fragrance that I remember still.

Some people threw cones on their night-fires but my parents considered that constituted a fire-risk and never practised it. Also risky was a friend's habit of waving a lighted twig round a room to sweeten the air. Never under any circumstances did we blow out a lamp; it was always extinguished by a careful lowering of the wick till it flickered out.

The changeable weather and frequent gales was the time we expected to see occasional rare bird-visitors which had been blown off course away from their normal migration routes; and we loved to see the sight of parent partridges marshalling their chicks across a road before our very eyes. One day swifts would be screaming as they ranged higher and higher in the sky, next day they would be gone, not to be seen again till next summer. The cuckoo would have gone long ago, and most of the birds had ceased their singing.

Nowhere could the silence be felt more than on the hills and moors where the red grouse whirred up hastily almost from under our feet, followed by an almost fully-grown brood. There was still the muted cooing of wood pigeons, and sometimes a disturbed cock pheasant soared overhead, topping the tall trees in his frenzied flight.

The woods were ablaze with colour and the hills were purple with the heather that is the symbol of Scotland the world over; many of its ancient uses are now forgotten. Ropes of heather were once in use in every clachan; cottages were thatched with it and every box-bed had its mattress filled with the springy flowers. Clansmen who slept in the open, as they were often obliged to do, would collect a quantity of heather, than arrange themselves in rows and, covered by their plaids, they thatched themselves with the heather; apparently the keenest frost did them no harm.

The Picts in the sixth century brewed a famous ale from a 'receipt' which had been handed down from father to son for generations. Even under threat of death they refused to reveal the secret recipe which legend says died with them. It was to this legend that Robert Louis Stevenson referred when he wrote

> From the bonny bells of heather
> They brewed a drink langsyne
> Was sweeter far than honey
> Was stronger far than wine.

Borderers are said to call bell heather 'she' heather, and ling they call 'he' heather.

The Glen main road was rich in ferns. We also picked the yellow mountain violet, the Alpine Lady's Mantle, and the tormentil which Cheviot shepherds call the ewe daisy. In boggy places we found the Grass of Parnassus, a slender plant with large white flowers, and also the bog asphodel, its wiry stems topped with orange-yellow flowers.

When the whin seeds were ripe and ready to scatter we distinctly heard the rattle of black pods bursting like tiny pistol shots in quick succession. Later this was repeated by the pods of yellow broom which grew in great stretches along the Deeside road — as we passed along the black pods were popping all over the place.

Wild berries were plentiful among the hills. The averin grew very high up beyond the reach of all but shepherds and climbers. The cranberry was a berry of the peat-mosses. Not so very long ago cottage women would spend a long day on the hills picking cranberries for jam, bringing home between them at the end of the day a clothes-basket full.

Blaeberries grew freely on the lower slopes, even by the roadside near the Manse, where we picked them for jam, getting hands and lips stained purple in the process, not to mention purple-stained pinafores.

The small black crowberry was rather astringent; we found it growing plentifully among the heather, fairly low down, but we did not eat any — we felt that they were strictly for the birds.

Wild rasps flourished on waste ground; they were small and delicious, and jam made from them had a specially fine flavour. Unfortunately, with so much road-widening, bushes of wild rasps have practically disappeared from familiar waysides.

When the rich purple-black berries of the elder tree were hanging in clusters like inverted umbrellas on their red stalks between the leaves, our Scots great-great-grandmothers, who believed that the fruit had healing properties, made elderberry wine, and elderberry syrup which they used to cure coughs; it was also delectable when added to sauces. They used the fruit in a number of other ways – in puddings and pies, in chutney, jam and jelly. They even dried the berries by hanging them up in butter-muslin in a warm place, afterwards storing them in jars. These, they said, were good to chew, or to brew like tea to ward off a cold. Today, if you should wish to make a drink endearingly called 'Cuddle-ma-dearie', you must add three parts green ginger wine to one part whisky – no cold can resist it!

On some of the lovely days we went exploring. I recall a picnic on a grassy bank beside the Quoich surrounded by autumn-tinted foliage; the sun flooded down warming the drystane dyke at our backs, glinting on the tumbling water. Near us was the wide golden sweep of a cornfield and a little breeze stirred the ripe ears into a long slow whisper, mingling with it the scent of a thousand growing things. We returned home happy though weary, pushing our bikes up the steep hill road while the last rays of the sun were fading in the western sky and brown owls swept on velvet wings from the darkening woods.

Pushing our way up the Torbeg Brae after a late evening with friends the road was bathed in silver light when the moon came up. When the old house with its archway of rowans loomed ahead, grey and silver, there was a glint of yellow where a moonbeam touched a window of the porch. Later in the season the rowantrees were almost stripped of leaves though they clung to their clusters of berries, red and ripe, soon to be harvested by the birds. The trees in the woods were almost bare, but the last copper and gold leaves clung to the tracery of black branches and touched to beauty the sombre paths where they fell.

We walked through piles of the dry fallen leaves that crackled under our feet. There was sometimes a night of severe frost when every blade of grass on the lawn held a stiff sheath of rime.

The horseman's job on a farm was one no tractor-driver would envy. Horses required long hours of attention in addition to those spent at work in the fields. Left out at night to graze, they had to be caught and brought back to the stable for a feed before going to work. In autumn and winter this preliminary job had to be done before daylight — no joke on a cold wet morning. The horseman invariably fed his horses before he himself fed; at lowsin' time in late afternoon it was the same procedure — horses and man went back to the stable, the horses to be fed and cared for before the man went home to his tea.

Corn was cut by the horse-drawn reaping machine, and the sheaves eventually carted to the stack yard. This was known as 'leading'.

Another seasonal task of former days was to bring in cart-loads of the gathered crop of potatoes to the 'tattie-pits' at the edge of the field, and make sure they were adequately protected under a mound of earth and straw against the severe weather that was bound to come.

After the leading came the biggin' o' the rucks, which were round in shape with a conical top. They were raised off the ground on stones to let air circulate and keep the stack dry and ventilated. Their bases were laid wheel-fashion with the cut end of the sheaves facing outward, and the grain inside. A man had to kneel to build the stack up gradually.

> O' for a day at the hint o' Hairst
> Wi' the craps weel in an' stackit
> Fan the fermer steps thro' the corn-yaird
> An' coonts a' the rucks he's thackit.

So wrote Charles Murray, the Donside poet, dreaming of Alford when far away in the Transvaal; but that was long ago.

Cream Crowdie was a special dish to celebrate the hint o'
hairst. Mary Ann Hay served Cream Crowdie to all the
helpers in the harvest fields at Ardoch, when the last load of
golden sheaves had been safely gathered in. She called it Fro'
Milk, but it was actually cream beaten to a stiff froth with a
fro'ing stick, and sweetened, with lightly toasted oatmeal
stirred in, which gave it a delicate nutty flavour.

In the Scottish Museum of Antiquities in Edinburgh may
be seen one of the old fro'ing sticks, which has a wooden
cross at the beating end, surrounded with a ring of cow's
hair. Many years ago I was given an identical stick by Janet
Ritchie of An Torran, complete with its wooden cross ringed
by a calfie's tail.

No longer does the farmer count his rucks, nor do men and
horses spend long hard-working days in dismantling stooks
and 'leading' the sheaves to the stack-yaird.

Threshing (or thrashing, as it was called) was of the utmost
importance; without it, neither man nor beast could be fed.
At the time of my earliest recollections, it was all done by
flail.

At one time horse-mills were an essential part of a small
farm's economy, replacing the weary business of threshing
by the flail (a scene I often witnessed) and allowed larger
quantities of grain to be threshed. I often saw horse-mills in
action at Balno and An Torran, and vaguely remember a
horse-mill at the Manse. There was no sign of it in the interior
of the barn, but behind the barn could be seen the circular
walk, raised above the level of the surrounding ground, and
the rotting remains of the horizontal crossed wooden beams
to which a single horse had been yoked as it walked round
and round. There were at one time a number of water-mills
in Glen Gairn, where the corn was ground by enormous
stones which revolved as a huge wheel drove round and

round. Those at Stranlea, Kirkstile, Tullich-ma-carrick with Millcroft across the water, and Laggan, 'the little hollow', have long been silent. Now the last of them, the Mill o'Prony, has ceased to function. It fascinated a child to see large quantities of oats being pounded into meal by the huge mill-stone, while outside rumbled the thirteen-foot mill-wheel, drawing its power from a well-built mill-lade.

Dr Maitland Mackie recently remarked that the passing of the threshing-mill typifies the change that has come over agriculture in the last fifty years. 'It used to take fourteen men to have a good "thrash",' he said, 'two to fork the sheaves from the ruck to the mill ... two to cut the straw band and pass the sheaf to the man who fed the mill (there were two who took turns in feeding the mill and looking after the steam engine). Other two strong men stood by to weigh the grain and carry it to a shed ready for loading. A lad was generally employed to sweep up the chaff and keep the mill clear. The straw meantime was gathered as it slid off the mill, and experts in building rucks began their work in the stack-yard. The engine had to be kept going with a steady supply of coal and water, and that was the work of yet another man. Several farmers joined together on thrashing-days, and with their combined efforts, and all the men they could muster, the job was completed.' It was very heavy work to carry through in a day (for the threshing-mill was booked to move to another farm next day), and specially heavy for the men whose job was to bag the grain, weigh it, and stack it ready for transport to the meal-mill at a later date.

The year wore on to Hallowe'en, the last night of the Celtic year when spirits from the other world were believed to revisit their old home, and witches, too, were abroad. Much folk-lore was recalled round many a fire-side, and young folk indulged in traditional ploys.

When Hallowe'en was safely over we had to settle down and prepare to face the freezing we would have to endure with chattering teeth before Christmas; but the worst weather generally came after the New Year.

# VII
# Clans and Clansmen

Come away, come away, Hark to the summons!
Come in your war array, Gentles and Commons,
Come every hill-plaid, and true heart that wears one,
Come every steel blade, and strong hand that bears one!

Sir Walter Scott

From its most primitive form of a hand-woven, undyed sort
of blanket made of sheep's wool, belted at the waist, and
carried over the head and shoulders when required, Highland
dress has developed into the most colourful and elaborate of
costumes.

Through time the early weavers learned how to dye their
cloth with the roots and bark of their native trees, with wild
flowers, bracken and lichen from stones on the hillside.

This is still being done to a certain extent by those who are
interested in preserving the ancient crafts. I remember May
Leys of Sleach, who spun and dyed her own sheep's wool to
the end of her days, once knitted me a pair of woollen gloves
which had been dyed a bright orange colour obtained from
bracken roots; and Catherine Neil in *Glengairn Calling*

describes a hand-woven wincey dress, striped in yellow and black, of which she was very proud. She herself had been delighted to gather the flowers of the ragwort from which the yellow dye was obtained for her new dress, and the common docken made a beautiful dye for the black stripes. (Today we marvel at the numberless patterns and colours woven in varied designs that make up the clan tartans and admire the knowledgeable who can recognise any or most of them at a glance.)

Down the ages every Highland family or clan came to have its own tartan by which it was recognised. There was the ordinary tartan worn by the ordinary members of the clan; there was a special tartan worn only by the Chief and his immediate heir; also the dress tartan which they wore only on occasions of state; and the hunting tartan for wear on the hills; lastly, there was the mourning tartan when the whole clan mourned the death of their Chieftain.

Besides the family tartan each clan had its own motto and badge. Into the badge on the bonnet was tucked an emblem of that clan — the Macdonalds of the Isles wore a sprig of heather, the Farquharsons a sprig of cranberry, and so on. The Frasers' emblem is yew and their motto is Je suis pret — I am ready.

In addition to its tartan and badges every clan still has its own battle-cry and pipe music — its march or pibroch, its gathering music and laments. A pibroch records some famous clan deed or victory, or the prowess of some chieftain. As the post of piper was hereditary, pibrochs have been handed down from father to son, and with them have come the traditions of the family, its past greatness, its success and failure, its history of joy and sorrow.

Today the wearing of the tartan is preserved in the uniform of the Highland Regiments in the British Army. In the South

African War, when the War Office ordered a transformation to khaki, there was nearly a mutiny and a compromise was reached by the authorities whereby khaki aprons were worn over the blue-black kilts of the Black Watch and the yellow striped kilts of the Gordon Highlanders. Since the wearing of tartan was made a transportation offence in 1747, the wearing of it has for Scots become a matter of conscience. Today it lives not only in the garb of Highland Regiments, but in the hereditary dress of clan pipers, and as the dress of retainers of some of the oldest Highland families.

Strictly speaking, only known members of a clan have the right to wear their clan tartan. However, we do find people who have no connection with a clan take a fancy to one for its blending of its colours and pattern, and enthusiastically invest in the whole costly outfit, kilt, doublet, plaid and all, adding the finest sporran they see, and a skean dhu to wear in their hose. This costume they are known to wear in all its glory at Highland gatherings and at Highland Balls, without troubling to learn that it is not fancy dress but a costume with a long and intensely interesting history.

In 1747, after the '45 Rising, a very severe Disarming Act was passed, prohibiting the carrying of arms, the playing of bagpipes, and the wearing of the kilt, the penalty for contravening the Act being a fine of £15 and six months' imprisonment, and for a second conviction, as already mentioned, transportation for life. The Act was repealed in 1782 and, to some extent, the old dress came back into general use.

When Queen Victoria first attended the Gathering of the Clans at Braemar with Prince Albert in 1848 she not only set the seal of success on the revival of such gatherings, but she restored Highland Games to their place of honour in Scottish tradition — a field of contest for kilted stalwarts who practise ancient sports. She was enthralled by everything

Highland — the tartans, the clans, piping and dancing, as well as the sports.

Autumn was, and still is, the season for all the great local gatherings — Braemar, Ballater, Aboyne, and the Lonach Gathering, which we happily attended, thrilling to the skirl of the pipes and the swagger of the kilt.

Fragments of an old ballad were found among family papers by Janet Ritchie of An Torran. It describes part of the Farquharson contingent mustering at Strath-Ley, the old name for Stranlea, before setting out to take part in the famous March of the Clansmen at Braemar. They were all Invercauld men, and wore the Farquharson tartan. Bremner of Strath-Ley is mentioned, and the 'brave John Coutts' of Tamnafeidh, also Macintosh of Brennaline, which we now know as Braenaloin. The last March of the Clansmen took place in 1936, but one old tradition has been revived — the race up Craig Choinnich instituted by Malcolm Canmore and stopped by Queen Victoria because of the strain it put upon the athletes was revived a couple of years ago in a more moderate form. From the arena at 1,100 feet the runners make their way up to the five cairns on Morrone at 2,600 feet before the descent to the arena for the finish in front of some 20,000 spectators.

In 1966 they put on a new event, the lifting on to a three-foot-high platform of the Inver Stone, which is an awkwardly-shaped granite boulder weighing 286 pounds. The first competitor to tackle it was a Crathie man, Norman Barbour, himself weighing only a little over eleven stone. With comparative ease he lifted the Stone on to the platform, and walked away with the Cup!

Legend has it that Malcolm Canmore was the instigator of Ghillie Callum, the Sword Dance, when on the occasion of a

96

celebration of a great victory in battle he placed his own sword over the sword of his vanquished enemy and danced over and round the crossed swords.

John Clark, a Crathie-born blacksmith, in Glenmuick, plied his trade on the royal estate for thirty-eight years, and was well-known to Queen Victoria and her family. They were frequent visitors to his smiddy at Ardmenach to see John hammer out horse-shoes at his forge. The Queen presented him with a complete outfit of Highland dress so that he could take part in the March of the Clansmen as a Balmoral Highlander at the Braemar Gathering. He knew her son, both as Prince of Wales and as King Edward VII. He was the King's oldest tenant on Deeside.

It has been asserted by the knowledgeable that only one young man in a thousand can with training hope to become a champion local athlete, and only one in ten thousand can aspire to first class honours in athletic contests. Robert Shaw, therefore, grandson of John Clark, was one in ten thousand. He was born at Inverenzie, the Laggan of Glen history; I remember him as an infant on his mother's knee.

He began at the age of seventeen to take part in local events at Braemar and at twenty-one was already coming to the fore as a hammer-thrower. It was predicted that he would be among the champions in the following season, and indeed, as Bob Shaw of Ballater, he became one of the leading 'heavies' in the country and held that position for twenty-five years. At one time Bob was Scotland's champion shot-putter. A natural athlete, he excelled also in tossing the caber and in Cumberland wrestling. He retired from contests after the Second World War and for years acted as a judge of heavy events at Highland gatherings all over the country. His sons, William and Robert, competed as boy-pipers at Braemar, and now his great-nieces, Anna and Lorraine, John Clark's great-great grand-daughters, carry on the family tradition as pipers and dancers with conspicuous success.

The long-held superstition that green is an unlucky colour to wear has both a practical and a superstitious origin. It seems that the first green dye produced commercially for colouring cloth had something poisonous in its composition and many wearers of the new green clothing were believed to have died through poison penetrating the pores of the skin, so green came to be an unlucky colour, an idea that must have died a natural death years ago. Yet four of the Scottish clans — the Grahams, Lindsays, Ogilvies and Sinclairs — had reason to regard green as unlucky for very different reasons. Bonnie Dundee was clad in green when he was killed at the Battle of Killiecrankie; the Lindsays were wearing green when they met with disaster at the Battle of Brechin; and the Ogilvies wore green at the Battle of Arbroath. Three hundred of the Sinclairs were wearing green uniforms when they crossed the Ord of Caithness on their way to Flodden, and only seven men returned from that disastrous battle-field.

When grouse-driving began a few days after the Glorious Twelfth of August, the women-folk took over the daily jobs on the farms, including the care of the beasts, for every fit man found temporary employment as a loader or as a gillie, and every boy old enough to stand up to a long day on the hill was engaged as a beater at a few shillings a day; at the end of the shooting season it was hoped their earnings would provide them with new tweed suits — jacket, waistcoat, and short trousers — and strong winter boots. They set out early in the morning with a 'piece' in their pocket, assembling at a given point. When the keeper gave the signal they moved off in line, each in his appointed place, waving his home-made white flag to keep the rising birds flying in the direction of the butts, which, in the Glen, were constructed of banked heathery turf about four feet high and forty yards apart in certain places on the hill. Behind them the 'guns' were concealed, waiting for the coming of the birds, and as these swept high overhead at sixty, seventy or more miles per hour this called for quick and accurate shooting. The Royal Butts above the quarry in the Delnabo wood were almost circular in shape with a small entrance and raised seats of turf. The children made a point of climbing the hill after a shoot to collect as souvenirs the empty cartridge-cases that lay around.

Mary Smith and Janet, her white pony, were engaged to go to the hill to bring down the game.

One lad who was always at the grouse-driving was Jock, an orphan brought up by Mrs Grant at Shenval. When school-days were over, and boys promoted to long trousers, most boys sought employment on distant farms, for the Glen had little to offer them. Jock, however, was content to remain in the neighbourhood, doing ditching and other casual jobs. He often called at Stranlea for a chat and a cup of tea. His characteristic expressions are still remembered and enjoyed. 'Fat's adee wi' yer beets?' translated means 'What's wrong with your boots?' The suggestion to 'cut it' to Jock, seen wrestling with a knotted piece of string, brought the reasoned reply 'A'm sweir tae cut the gweed tow', meaning 'I'm unwilling to cut the good string'.

In course of time Jock became bell-ringer and beadle at the kirk, and proudly 'took up the collection'. On one occasion, in the absence of the organist, he even tried to play the American organ. The minister had called for a volunteer and Jock, who had always thought it looked very easy, confidently came forward, sat down and proceeded to finger the keys.

Alas! His chords were all lost ones, and amid the cacophony of sound the minister gently implored him to stop. His latter years as a labourer on the Balmoral Estate were spent in a bothy at Abergeldie, where he considered himself custodian of the Castle. Now, in his old age, clean-shaven and well-dressed, with regular meals in a comfortable Home, Jock, I am happy to say, is in better shape than he was in the whole of his working life.

The kennels at Rinloan were the responsibility of Donald Fraser, the keeper. They consisted of long narrow compartments, with a large run, surrounded by high railings. When one passed along the road the whole four-footed rabble rushed to the front and cannonaded with a full orchestra of barking, with wet noses poking through the bars. When we met Donald out with his gun, from which no gamekeeper on duty was ever parted, his invariable cheerful greeting, no matter the weather, was 'It's a gran' day tae be oot on the hull'.

Postie, who lived at Rinloan, walked daily to and from Ballater, carrying and delivering letters, and, reluctantly, the occasional parcel. In those days, telegrams were sent to the folk in the Glen only in cases of extreme urgency, and, all too often, the orange-coloured envelope contained bad news. A boy was sent from Ballater Post Office on a red bicycle to deliver it for a small charge. He wore a smart uniform of navy serge with a pill-box hat, and a leather belt with a purse stitched into it in which he carried the telegram.

After Prince Albert's death the Queen tended to prolong her visits to Balmoral. She would stay from May to June, return in August and stay till mid-November. This she continued to do almost to the end of her long reign. Balmoral was Paradise to her but to her Ladies in Waiting a spell of duty there was a dreary experience and a test of endurance. The Queen had remarkably good circulation, and a thirty-five-mile drive in an open carriage on a frosty afternoon left her only surprised that her knees felt stiff. She drove around in a pony carriage accompanied by one of her ladies. The small phaeton could be driven on narrow roads and bridle-paths in remote parts of the Balmoral Forest where no ordinary carriage could go. John Brown always attended the carriage on foot and a gillie led the pony.

Princess Alice, Countess of Athlone, even in her nineties, had undimmed memories of staying at Balmoral with her grandmother, the Queen, who insisted that her guests accompany her on picnics, whatever the weather. The Princess told of driving with her grandmother one very wet day when both got soaked to the skin.

Nothing ever changed at Balmoral; fires were seldom lit in any of the rooms. After a five-year absence, Marie Mallet, a lady-in-waiting, wrote to a friend:

> I feel as if I had never been away; the same chairs are placed in the same corners — the same plum cake is served, even the same number of biscuits on a plate, and the same varieties appear; the same things are said, the same things done — only some of the old faces are gone, and new dogs follow the phaeton.

The Queen was very fond of Glashalt Shiel, her retreat at the head of Loch Muick. Once when returning from a long day at the Shiel the pony stumbled and the phaeton overturned. No one was hurt. John Brown assisted the Queen and her friend to regain their feet and then cut the traces to release the pony.

Miss Abercrombie, a kinswoman of my friend Margaret Robbie, was Housekeeper at Glashalt Shiel. James Abercrombie, who followed Arthur Grant as Head Stalker at Balmoral, was Margaret's father, and John Robbie, Head Stalker at Glenmuick, and later Head Gardener, was her husband's father, two families with generations in Royal Service.

I recently learned the story of the piping Browns.

Robert Brown as a little lad loved to listen to bagpipes; his uncles were grand pipers and he was eager to learn to play. His sister, Bessie, was also keen but she, a sufferer from polio, was confined to a wheel-chair. So close were brother and sister that every day when Robert came home from his piping lesson he showed Bessie the chanter, the reeds, and other parts of the bagpipes, telling her what he had learned that day. During the long hours when Bessie sat alone she handled her brother's pipes, and tried to master the intricacies of fingering and rhythm.

Years passed and Robert became one of the finest pipers in the land. To the end of his life he was the Queen's Piper who played round Balmoral Castle every morning, and on all special occasions.

Learning about piping had opened the door to a new way of life for Bessie. She, too, became famous, recognised as one of Deeside's top teachers of piping. For many years she was also a well-known judge of piping, and at nearly seventy, in spite of her disability, travelled widely from her home in Banchory.

Speaking of piping reminds me that King Edward VIII was the first British sovereign to play the bag-pipes. He was taught by Pipe-Major Henry Forsyth. Edward also composed a slow march for the pipes which he called 'Mallorca'.

Sandy Campbell was the deerstalker at Glashalt Shiel who set up what he called the Loch Muick Museum. He gathered a large number of curious objects from the surrounding hills: samples of the six-foot-high heather that grew alongside the torrent called the Glas Allt, or Grey Burn; pieces of rock crystal; cairngorm stones; fox-masks and the antlers of stags.

Another well-known local personality was Mrs Macnab, the wife of a Crathie farmer, a hospitable woman of natural charm and a light hand in the making of buttermilk scones. She often welcomed to her fireside King Frederick of Prussia and other distinguished guests at Balmoral who dropped in for a cup of tea in her spotless kitchen, and a scone fresh from the girdle.

# VIII
# Mountain Lore

To walk on the hills is to see sights and to hear sounds
    unfamiliar;
When in wind the pine-tree roars, when crags with
    bleating echo, when water foams beneath the fell
Hearts record that journey as memorable indeed.

Robert Graves

'You'll be lonely in the country now you've retired,' predicted city friends, and there are times when an acquaintance
will express surprise that I decline to put my feet up, but
continue to write; but how, otherwise, I ask, can I avoid
becoming a human cabbage? How occupy my days?

Shall I emulate some of my forebears and write innumer-
able letters to the *Scotsman* and the *Glasgow Herald*, or shall
I become a regular contributor to *Any Answers*? Besides,
whatever the disadvantages of life in the country, loneliness
is not one of them.

Quite apart from the friendliness and kindness of my
neighbours, my family, and old friends, many casual acquain-
tances and warm-hearted strangers find their way to my door.

Among them such personalities as Dr Adam Watson and Inspector Duff, Dr Nan Shepherd, Alastair Mackie, poet of the Nor' East, and May Thomson, surely one of the most kenspeckle figures not only in Aberdeen, but well beyond the 'Twa' Mile Roon' of the city. She is always willing to share her abiding passion of folk-lore in a highly entertaining way, and often held my delighted attention for an entire afternoon while she recited with dramatic effect and equal fluency impromptu selections from the poems of David Rorie, Charles Murray, Douglas Young, and Flora Garry.

Nesta Bruce, my friend and fellow-student of Dunfermline College days, also visited me when we were older and (perhaps) wiser. Even in her schooldays Nesta was a daring gymnast and strong swimmer, who regularly dived into and swam the harbour at Fraserburgh, her home town, and even swam Fraserburgh Bay. Many years later her cousin, George Bruce, who has been teacher, BBC producer, poet and first Fellow of Creative Writing at Glasgow University, and Professor of English at Wooster College, Ohio, recalled how when he was a small boy, Nesta taught him to swim. In his own words, 'When she said to me in the peremptory manner of the teacher of physical education (which she was), "take hold of my arm", I did so unquestioningly. She pulled me a long way out, then shook herself free and said, in effect, "All Bruces swim – now SWIM". I swam.'

To all I give a warm greeting and speed them on their way with a hearty 'Haste ye back' which means 'Come again soon'.

One fine day in August, when the air was filled with the mingled scents of pine and thyme, George and Norma Mackie and the boys called for me in their Land Rover. They had heard me express a wish to see Auchtavan, the remote sheiling beloved of the Queen Mother, and that was to be the object of our outing.

Over the steep Stranyarroch we went, with a grand view of Lochnagar before dipping down past Piperhole into Crathie. Leaving Balmoral behind secluded in its wooded grounds, we turned off the Deeside road at the old Mill of Inver, where the Fearder Burn joins the River Dee — the burn that long ago was haunted by a fearsome spectre of a black hairy hand severed at the wrist. For generations the centuries-old mill was tenanted by a family called Davidson, and one dark and wintry night in 1777 John Davidson saw the floating apparition of the Black Hand while he was working in the mill. He immediately challenged it and although he would never divulge what took place it seems that he had a fierce encounter with something. The following morning he was seen digging in a corner of his garden where he eventually unearthed the basket-hilt of a broadsword. This hung for many years over the fireplace in the mill; and the apparition which had long terrorised the local inhabitants of Glen Fearder was never seen again. We followed the Aberarder road as far as the little kirk (now in ruins) where the Rev. S.J. Ramsay Sibbald, Chaplain to the Queen, held occasional services, and where Chae Downie, a prosperous sheep farmer, now stores hay for the winter feeding of his considerable flock. Aberarder was once the property of the Earls of Mar. For centuries their tenants were the Farquharsons of Invercauld and their kinsmen the Shaws of Rothiemurchus. There were also a number of bonnet lairds, always quarrelling among themselves or fighting a common enemy. Weary of this unhappy state of affairs, the Farquharsons invited all the bonnet lairds to a meeting in the Great Barn at Aberarder, and hanged eighteen of them from the roof tree. One escaped to tell the grim story, and there was no more clan-strife in

Aberarder! The Farquharsons have owned the land since 1745.

We crossed the burn by a little bridge near the isolated farm-house of Belmore, and glimpsed a roe deer as we entered a wood and followed a track winding upward among the birches, emerging at last on a grassy plateau. We were now at the head of Glen Fearder, 'the glen of high water', in sight of Auchtavan, the only house left standing there 1,500 feet above sea-level. The name, from the Gaelic meaning 'the field of the kids', is a reminder that in the days of feudal practice, part of the rent paid to the Laird had been in the shape of two young goats. Many scattered larachs showed where once had been a tiny oasis of cultivation and an active community. Fenton Wyness describes it as a 'truly mysterious region possessing a strange fascination for those susceptible to atmosphere'.

We actually found ourselves conversing in whispers; even the children were silent. I imagined I heard a distant piper, and Douglas Young's lines on the old Highlands came to mind:

> The old lonely loving way of living . . .
> Peaceful bounty flowing
> Passed like the dust blowing,
> That harmony of folk and land is shattered,
> Peat-fire and music, candlelight and kindness . . .
> Now they are gone
> And desolate these lovely lonely places.

The solitude was impressive, and the view across the valley to the cobalt blue bulk of Lochnagar and the neighbouring hills was superb.

In such a setting one could not fail to recall how a lone climber in the Cairngorms relates how, one August evening in the Larig Ghru, the sun had just disappeared behind the great peaks, and a strange uncanny silence came with the approach of twilight. Suddenly he heard bagpipes, a slow melody like a lament.

When he arrived at the Corrour Hut he expected to find a piper there, and was amazed to find the hut unoccupied. The haunting strains accompanied him till nightfall. Nothing will ever convince him that he did not hear a ghostly piper in the lonely vastness of that mountain pass.

Reluctantly turning away from those patches of forgotten fields, we passed on to a track used mainly by climbers and shepherds, part of an ancient hill-road which in recent times has been widened and roughly maintained for the convenience of shooting-parties. There is even a primitive wooden building to house hill-ponies overnight so that they may be on the spot ready for the following day's shoot. Mountain hares can be thin on the ground in the Cairngorms, but that evening they were darting everywhere. The sight of another hare running, or the alarm call of grouse will alert a hare and send it tearing away without waiting to see the cause of the alarm. The Land Rover, rocking its way along the track, which in some parts resembled a dried-up river-bed, disturbed not only hares, but rabbits, sheep, deer, and an occasional grouse. The Laird and a party had been out from Invercauld that day, walking with dogs, and the grouse they had bagged would be collected by a game-dealer in the morning.

Never before had I seen so many herds of antlered stags, hinds, and calves, not quietly feeding, undisturbed by our presence, as we had often seen in Glen Muick, but fleeing in alarm. Before Norma could adjust her camera they were out of range. Seton Gordon describes how one August morning he stood high above Glen Giusachan and saw an immense herd of stags and hinds feeding on a sheltered grassy slope.

The whole hill-face was covered with deer, like a vast flock of sheep from his distant view-point. The majority were feeding, and he marvelled at the quantity of grass that must have been consumed by that herd in the course of a single day.* Hinds are watchful and suspicious at all times and will prick up their ears at the slightest sound, giving a yelping bark as a warning signal to the whole herd. Calves have a high-pitched call rather like the bleat of a goat. George told me there is no authentic record of a hind having more than one calf at a time, though one may occasionally be seen suckling the year-old calf and the baby at the same time. He had no sooner spoken when the boys and I were thrilled to see a hind galloping away at great speed with two calves loping along at her side.

The stony track, dipping at times at alarming angles, continued to wind along the hillside. Only George's expert handling of the Land Rover kept it on course; there was a rocky gully several feet deep a few inches from the edge, but George, unperturbed, was used to such tracks when gathering sheep. Far away were the windswept heights of Ben Macdhui, which looks like a great black pig, and is mentioned in a tale of a legendary boar-hunt.

The existence, or presence, of the spectre known as the Grey Man of Ben Macdhui has been vouched for by a considerable number of reliable people — novice climbers and veteran mountaineers — over the years. The appearance of the figure and the experience of the climbers vary. Footsteps

*In 1925 Seton Gordon kindly permitted me to have lantern slides made from photographs in his *Cairngorm Hills of Scotland*. I particularly value one which shows him seated on the top of Brae Riach, spying the Larig Ghru through his long glass, wearing, as always, his kilt and bonnet, and smoking his pipe.

are heard sometimes crunching in the snow behind them, sometimes a gigantic figure is seen walking on the summit, at times a loud weird cry is heard, but in all cases terror overtakes them.

An early report came from a Professor at London University in 1891; since then reports have come at intervals, including the years 1904, 1914, 1928 and 1942. The presence is felt at different hours of the day and night, in mist and bright sunshine alike. These strange happenings have convinced learned men that something out of the ordinary, to put it mildly, does take place from time to time on the wild and stony slopes of Ben Macdhui.

Climbing steeply, we came, to my surprise and great joy, upon the infant Gairn, just over a mile from its source on Ben A'an, that mountain of many summits and little streams, and in its heart the Lochan nan Gabhar, the Lochan of the Goats.

Beside the Gairn oyster-catchers were piping, for even in August they still look after their young, and are often heard in the upland glens where snow lies even in May. Not far away we heard the mournful cry of a plover. When the river began to widen we came down to its level and crossed it by a well-made bridge. The valley opened out, and we were almost in sight of Loch Builg. On just such a lonely spot, at his cottage on the edge of a moor miles from anywhere, Ronald Macdonald Douglas had a petrifying experience. He often heard bagpipes, but could never locate a piper. Then, late one night, he heard sounds of battle, the clash of steel on steel, men yelling, and, above all the clashing and shouting, the wild skirl of the pipes. He rose from bed and went out, wondering what he would find. His dogs cringed, trembling. There was the sound of marching men but nothing to be seen.

Nearer and nearer came the ghost-army. Ronald actually *felt* it pass within a few yards of him, accompanied by the ranting pipes. Then the army passed *clean through the house*, and went off towards the south. He heard it fade into the night; long after, he discovered that the hill from which had come the battle-noises is known locally as Mam a Catha, the Hill of the Battle.

Three old highland roads meet at Loch Builg and continue as a path to Inchrory and Tomintoul. Inchrory stands at a cross-roads. It was the meeting-place of the drove roads from the north by the Avon to Gairnside, Braemar, and Donside, as well as something of a bottle-neck for the reiving traffic of the seventeenth and eighteenth centuries. Loch Builg lies two and a half miles south of Inchrory, and the old drove road by the burn, between the loch and Inchrory, is a delightful walk, rich with limestone flowers. There is fine grazing all along the east side of the glen, which provided overnight pasture for droves of cattle and sheep, the drovers finding shelter under some of the bigger juniper bushes.

Margaret Fraser of Balno recalls that her forebears, the Shaws, who had been tenants of Inchrory and Glen Builg since 1745, returned to Abernethy in 1841, whence the family originally came to Gairnside in 1716.

On an old flat stone in the churchyard of Rothiemurchus are five curious stones, roughly cylindrical like petrified cheeses, such as were made in the crofts long ago. They may possibly have been supports on which the flat stone once rested. It is the grave of Farquhar Shaw, who led thirty men of his clan to defeat the Davidsons of Invernahaven on the North Inch at Perth in 1396. He was the son of Alexander Shaw of Rothiemurchus. Descendants of this Farquhar were called

Farquharsons. In their early history the name of Finlay Mor is prominent. He was standard-bearer at the Battle of Pinkie, where he fell in 1547. There is a legend that if any of the five stones on Farquhar Shaw's grave is removed it will return of its own accord and disaster will overtake the culprit within a year.

When the Duchess of Bedford was staying nearby in the autumn of 1830, one of her footmen, Robert Scroggie, removed a stone and threw it into the Spey. He was ordered to put it back but was drowned in the river a few days later. Two other men are known to have removed stones from the grave and to have died within the year.

There was an exciting occurrence in the neighbourhood of quiet Tomintoul in June 1920. An abandoned stone cottage was the scene of the last-but-one episode in what was then known as the Topliss Affair. In April that year Percy Topliss, an ex-soldier, shot a taxi-driver in Andover and disappeared. Some time later a man appeared in Tomintoul and took up his quarters in the lonely hillside cottage. Little notice was taken of him till he was seen to be tearing down the wood-work for firewood. The Tomintoul policeman, accompanied by two neighbours, called at the cottage where they were received by revolver shots and two of them were wounded. The man fled and from his description it became clear that he must be Topliss who had, in some fashion, found his way from Hampshire to that remote spot in the Banffshire Highlands. Nothing more was heard of him for five days, when he was spotted walking on the road between Carlisle and Penrith in Cumbria. When challenged by a policeman he drew his revolver; the policeman sought armed assistance and a large number of men turned out to help the police. After a search and a skirmish, Topliss was shot in a field near Plumpton.

For long Glenlivet has had peat-cutting rights on a moor near Tomintoul, and in earlier times seasonal employment for women was cutting peats for the distillery. They walked to and from their work, and were paid one shilling and sixpence for *a ten-hour day*.

Whisky smugglers, their ponies laden with kegs of The Real Glenlivet, crossed the Lecht hills by various routes in order to avoid the attention of the gauger and his men, but the recognised 'whisky road' from the Braes of Glenlivet was a track much used in olden days by the local folk on their lawful occasions.

Loch Builg with its curving stretch of sandy beach, is a pleasant spot for a picnic on a sunny day as my friends, the Ritters, discovered one summer. They ate their lunch by the boat-house where, over eighty years ago, Charlie Anderson, a Ballater business-man, kept his cabin-cruiser. The picnic party was watched at surprisingly close quarters by a herd of inquisitive red deer on the hillside, forgetting all fear in their intent examination of the human invaders. From Loch Builg, we in the Land Rover followed a winding road made familiar to me in letters from Jessie Barnes and her husband, who are tireless walkers. We remarked that the surface was a great improvement on the Bealach Dearg, and we shortly came upon Corndavon, once a shooting-lodge, now roofless, except for one room where the window has been restored, the walls pointed, and a snug little picnic corner created for the Queen Mother. The attractive murals are still in good order, but the Queen Mother no longer rents the Corndavon land held by the Laird of Invercauld.

In my childhood days Corndavon Lodge was let every season. Lord Cardigan, of Crimean reputation, was the tenant for some years; much later the tenant was Mrs Inge, a fine horsewoman, adored by Maggie Cumming the housekeeper, who was at all times ready to show off the house and its treasures, which included some of the beds still draped in faded tartan said to have been in the fray at Culloden. Lord Belper was almost the last shooting tenant of Corndavon. His daughter, Lavinia, married the Duke of Norfolk.

When we reached Daldownie I was saddened to see that the shepherd's sturdy cottage where John Thomson was born is now reduced to a pile of rubble. John emigrated to Canada and became an exploration engineer and geologist in the service of the Dominion Government. For over forty years he explored the High Arctic Territories. There is, he maintains, no road, railroad, or airfield that he did not locate and build, including the DEW line, that is the Distant Early Warning Line for the American Government from Herschel Island to King William's Land. This comprised a series of radar-spotting stations all along the Arctic Coast of Canada, intended to give early warning to the Americans of any Russian missiles. Many of the stations have long been abandoned, but the airfields are still useful.

Now a consultant living in Yellowknife, the capital of the North West Territories, John has always loved the Arctic and the Barren Lands, which in many ways remind him of Scotland. He has taken a prominent part in the planning of a new site in Yellowknife which will approximately double its present population. He was engaged by the Canadian Government to adjudicate in mineral claims on Cornwallis Island, and by the Government of Alberta to settle boundary disputes south of Calgary; he was also commissioned to divide the North West Territories into two electoral divisions, without interfering with the traditional hunting grounds of Eskimo families.

At a recent reception given by the Commissioner and the Government, John and his wife were presented with the

Commissioner's highest award for their joint contribution to the welfare and progress of the community of Yellowknife in particular, and of the North West Territories in general.

Standing on the bridge at Daldownie my thoughts returned to fishing trips of long ago when my husband and I and our family got fine baskets of speckled trout from the Daldownie pools. Now one can only approach that territory on foot, for a locked gate bars the way for vehicles. On this occasion we had been provided with a key by David Guild, the game-keeper at Crathie. The bridge at Daldownie is said to be the identical bridge which was to have carried the railway over the river at Fit o' Gairn had the project not been abandoned. The biggest trout I ever landed was caught without skill or effort by dropping my line over that bridge. In the failing light we looked across to Sleach, and to Tullich-ma-Carrick, once the Manse of Glen Gairn, both standing empty.

James Neil was the elder son of the Rev. Robert Neil, my father's predecessor as parish minister. James was born, as were all the members of the family, in that Manse at the upper end of the parish. He graduated as a doctor, and devoted the whole of his professional life to the advancement of mental health. He was Medical Superintendent of a hospital in Oxford in his latter years. He was the author of *Ian Roy of Skellater, Soldier of Fortune*. He built the spacious house in Ballater which is now the Manse of Glenmuick, and there his sister, Catherine, wrote the charming booklet *Glen Gairn Calling*, which has achieved immense popularity.

Their younger brother, Robert, like James, received his early schooling from his father and from the old Dominie, James Coutts, at the Schoolhouse of Dalphuil, now a royal picnic cottage. Robert matriculated at Aberdeen University at the early age of fourteen. He had an extraordinary memory, and could memorise long passages after only brief study. He was a brilliant classical scholar, and became a Fellow and Tutor of Pembroke College, Cambridge. He was a student of Sanskrit, and with his friend, Professor Cowell, published translations of ancient Sanskrit papers, transcribing the original lettering into Roman characters. He was only forty-nine years of age when he died. His sisters were educated at the Ministers Daughters College (my old school) in Edinburgh, which was later re-named Esdaile after its founder.

Nearing the end of our mountain journey we came by the lost clachan of Loinahaun to the ruins of Auchentoul where lived Peter Fleming, one of the few to escape with his life from the carnage of Culloden for, after the battle, the wounded were butchered by order of the Duke of Cumberland. Out of that order grew the legend of the Curse of Scotland.

On the eve of the battle Prince Charlie's officers were quartered in Culloden House and, in a game of cards, a card went missing. The following night, after the battle, it was the Duke of Cumberland and his staff who occupied Culloden House. The Duke instructed an officer to send out detachments to search the woods for Highlanders who might be in hiding there, and destroy every man.

The officer declined to do this without written instructions, and the Duke, rising from the table to look for writing-paper, tripped on a rug and turned up the missing card. 'This will do,' he said, and scribbled the order on the face of it. Since then the Nine of Diamonds has been known as the Curse of Scotland.

On Culloden Moor now stands a cairn, and green mounds mark the graves of the men of different clans who died in that last pitched battle on Scottish soil in 1746. I remember one August day, many years ago, when the moor was still in its natural state, we, as a family, gathered armfuls of purple heather and heaped them in memoriam in place of flowers on the grave of the Fraser clansmen.

Ghostly clansmen are said to haunt the moor. Sometimes a shadowy form of a weary Highlander is seen in the gloaming near the cairn. Not long ago a woman tourist thought she saw a dead man in Stewart tartan lying on one of the mounds, and fled in distress from the scene.

On the last mile of our journey by Land Rover we came by Rinloan, Gairnshiel, and Delnabo ('the dell of the cows'), till we turned in at the gate of my cottage at nine o'clock.

So ended our excursion into the 'lovely lonely places', an enchanted evening that will live in my memory as long as I live, and I murmured (with Seton Gordon) as I said Good Night

> May your heart keep true to the peaks above;
> May your feet be sure on the hills you love;
> May the summer mist and the winter storms
> Never hide your path to the High Cairngorms.

# IX
# Winter and Rough Weather

When all around the wind doth blow
And birds sit brooding in the snow.
                                    Shakespeare

The face of Scotland's hills does not change very much even
with the changing seasons; some of them rank among the
oldest hills in the world and have had the same shape for
thousands of years. In winter, before the first snowfall, they
are bare, even bleak, but still magnificent.

All through the autumn the sheep were out on the hill-
slopes, or in the fields, depending on the weather, but
November was tupping time, a busy time for the sheep-
farmer. Ewes had to be picked to go with the rams — twenty
to twenty-five to the young ram-lambs of the previous year,
fifty to an older ram. Later, the different groups merged
again into one flock and were once more turned out on the
hill.

The trunks of some trees were then acquiring a crinkled
coat of silvery lichen; there were no wild flowers left bloom-
ing to relieve the greyness, but Ellie and I delighted in the

fragrance of wet beech leaves and bruised pine-needles and forgot for a time the scent and colour of summer flowers. The birches had long lost the golden shimmer of autumn and were brown and shrivelled parodies of their former glory. The first fierce gale would strip the trees and leave them gaunt and bare.

Snow fell early on the high hills. The peaks that had looked blue in the distance stood out white-capped and remote against the blue sky. We children revelled in the sight of the first snowflakes drifting down silently as thistledown. The leafless trees cast long shadows across the new-fallen snow in the avenue, spruces and pines breaking the all-over whiteness. To Ellie and me the hush of a snowfall, the blustering of night-winds, the sound of rain on fallen leaves, were wrapped in a mystery we were too young to appreciate. The woods were a white fairyland, every tree sparkling in the winter sunshine.

I remember the absolute stillness of the snowbound Glen. When a blizzard swept down from the hills the Gairn assumed a frozen splendour, covered with ice and snow. It muttered under its thick covering, a sinister grumbling unlike its normal cheerful chatter. As the months wore on the snow blanket thickened. When the river froze over completely the ice was at least two inches thick; the faint sound of running water was silenced, not to be released till the land was warmed again by the sun and winds of spring. There was no colour in the landscape, but it had a quiet dignity and a beauty all its own.

We had our share of Arctic conditions. Anyone who survives exposure in a blizzard will never forget the terrifying experience. I have remembered all my life the nightmare journey we, as a family, had in the blizzard which began on Boxing Day 1907 and raged for several days.

A prolonged snowstorm greatly added to the anxieties of the hill shepherd. He might lose some ewes in the deep snow, others might be weakened for lambing-time. Farm work out-of-doors came to a standstill — all daylight hours were devoted to getting food in for their farmstock, clearing paths around the farm that snowdrifts soon filled up again, and keeping up a good peat fire in the kitchen to cope with every recurring domestic problem. Heavy snowfalls also had a devastating effect on wild life. Thrushes and plover in particular suffered when deep snow covered all their sources of food. Long-tailed birds like the pheasant found themselves in trouble when they tried to roost in trees, their tail-feathers stiff and frozen. Hungry rooks could be seen around the stack-yards, digging into the stacks in their desperate hunt for food. Corn-stacks are now things of the past and rooks have lost that source of food, as have the smaller birds like robins and wrens who found bed and breakfast in the warm crevices of stacks. When the ground was only lightly sprinkled with snow the tracks of animals and birds could be seen and recognised — the jump of rabbits, the walk of a pheasant, and the hopping of blackbirds.

The deer came down from the high tops, their coats rough with frozen snow. After a long fruitless search for food, hunger drove them to the very doors of the farm-steading. When the undergrowth was obliterated red deer, starving for lack of food on their native hills, came down to strip the bark from trees; later, when the snow had vanished, the marks on the trees were noticeable high above ground level, reminders of the time when the countryside was muffled in deep snow.

In sheltered places the conifers were a beautiful sight, fantastically festooned and heavily laden. In open places where the wind whipped the snow into drifts, drystane dykes were completely hidden and snow lay deep around them.

When hard frost came we walked to the kirk through the fields at dyke-level, the crisp snow crunching under our feet.

Snow and high winds played havoc in the woods; spruces were overthrown but pines were not so easily uprooted. After a storm the woods were littered with pine branches that had been broken by the weight of snow.

As no baker's van could get up the Glen road owing to deep snow, my mother made oven bread from a scone mixture; there was no scarcity of flour, or meal for our porridge, for the girnal had been filled in anticipation of such a familiar situation. When we could not go to the farm for fresh milk we used tinned condensed milk, a creamy substance of the consistency of golden syrup.

We were always warmly clad but had nothing in the way of waterproof clothing. As small children we did have little fur-lined snow-boots, and in our school-days rubber goloshes which fitted over our sturdy boots. We were 'snowed up', every year for weeks – even months – and never knew the phenomenon of an 'open' winter.

The clear frosty air carried sounds for miles and the surrounding hills acted superbly as an echo chamber. We clearly heard the voices of people passing along the road across the Water of Gairn; it was even possible by speaking 'loud and clear' to carry on a conversation with them, or to send an urgent message to a neighbouring farm.

Fixing the date of the night of the Christmas Tree entertainment, the great event of the school year, was a tricky business involving much earnest consultation regarding the phases of the moon. It was invariably held on the Friday in November nearest the full moon; this was important when miles of rough tracks over moorland had to be negotiated by many of the parents and children in darkness lightened only by the inadequate flicker of a stable lantern. I remember walking home afterwards — the woods and the hills and the silence, and above us the moon and a myriad of stars. In those days all our Christmasses were white, so the wisdom of holding the School Christmas Tree in November before the onset of winter weather was apparent.

There are so many legends associated with Christmas that it is difficult to sift fact from fiction. One popular fallacy is that crackers originated from the fear of evil spirits which were supposed to be abroad at that time, and loud noises were created to scare them away. Actually, it all began when Tom Smith was a confectioner's apprentice. He was a bright lad and gradually saved enough money to set up in business for himself. Ever on the look-out for new confections, he noticed in Paris a shopkeeper making pretty parcels of his bonbons, and was inspired to copy the idea. He bought a stock of coloured paper, and a quantity of sugared almonds from the famous shop in the Champs Elysées. Home again, his assistants were soon busily tying up sweets in the style we now recognise as the cracker-shape. They sold so well that he set about finding ways to make his sweet-packages even more attractive. The inspiration that made the cracker came when he was sitting at home and threw a log on the fire which began to crackle and pop. This made him sit up and take notice.

After repeated experiments he produced the means of causing a tiny explosion when the cracker was torn apart. Through time, he left out the sugared almond and substituted a small present. Tom Smith was the first cracker-man. His ideas were widely copied and cracker-making became a thriving industry.

In my childhood we received and sent to friends a large number of Christmas cards and calendars. In those days a card could be posted in an unsealed envelope for a halfpenny, and a letter cost only one penny. The same letter costs today the equivalent of thirty pennies.

The story of the first Christmas card is well-known; the history of the calendar is equally interesting.

It seems that as early as 4000 BC the Egyptians introduced the first calendar, so my father told us children. He was always willing to impart knowledge at appropriate moments. The Greeks had many calendars, he said, but the one accepted by the world for well over a thousand years was a version of the Egyptian calendar adopted by Julius Caesar.

The version we are using now is the Gregorian Calendar, reformed by Pope Gregory in the sixteenth century, and spurned in this country for 200 years because of its Roman origin.

In the seventeenth century calendars and almanacs seemed to spring up like mushrooms after rain. Gentlemen wore inside their top hats a calendar printed on a cardboard circle. The almanacs contained weather forecasts and other predictions by the astrologers of the day. Sometimes even more unexpected information was offered; in 1659 a 'Student of Physick' told prospective parents how to tell the sex of their unborn child by counting the letters in their Christian names and dividing the number by seven. An even number predicted the arrival of a girl, if uneven they might expect a boy.

One calendar which contained a table showing the current prices of food advised housewives to buy meat on Saturday night when butchers sold, cheaply, meat that would not keep till Monday. In those days a joint of veal or lamb could be purchased at that late hour for threepence a pound, which earlier in the day would have cost sevenpence per pound!

It was in 1816 that the first ruled and dated notebook for recording daily events and engagements was produced by John Letts, a printer and stationer. It was the cycle of events culminating in the defeat of Napoleon at Waterloo that inspired him to produce a book of this kind. We buy Mr Letts's Diaries and receive them in their infinite variety to this day.

From the hoard of a confirmed collector of newspaper clippings I borrowed a letter from the War Office dated September 1916, addressed to Dear Sir or Madam of the general public. Stripped of its pedantic language and much circumlocution, it invites readers to support a scheme for providing Christmas Puddings for the troops serving overseas by sending contributions to a fund sponsored by certain newspapers and recognised by the Army Council.

It advises readers not to send puddings to individual soldiers or special units as delivery cannot be guaranteed. Readers are assured that all puddings sent through the Fund will be of excellent quality, and 'subject to official inspection at every stage of their manufacture', well-packed and dispatched through military channels, so that every officer and man will receive half a pound of pudding to eat with his Christmas Dinner.

The letter is written by an anonymous gentleman who signs himself Your Obedient Servant.


My friend Iain Wilkinson, whose father was the Episcopal parson in Ballater, told me that he met the future Admiral Beatty and his American wife when they were living in Braemar Castle. He also told me that it was in Ballater that Sir William Beveridge with Principal Murray of the University College of the South West (now Exeter University) and Professor Findlay Shirras, the economist, drew up the grand design of the Welfare State. Iain was of the opinion that the scheme put an end to much of a Briton's pride in his independence.

He always thought it was a pity that Ballater did not have a newspaper to record events for posterity. In the 1920s a sort of broadsheet was produced in the summer, aimed at visitors. It contained mostly the names of holiday-makers and a few trifling items of news. Later on Henry Munro, who owned the Aberdeen *Bon Accord* and other weekly newspapers, considered the possibility of publishing a Dee-Don Echo, but after looking at the population figures, the cost of correspondence and the transport, he rejected the idea. But the *Bon Accord* gave good coverage to Deeside in its day. Now, unhappily, it has gone.

To those who love words for their shape and rhythm as well as for their meaning, there is a certain charm in the word 'candlelight' a spell to exorcise winter gloom, mellow and infinitely beautiful. Candlelight is the perfect accompaniment to the gentle brilliance of old brass. Lamps in endless variety have come and gone, but many a brass candlestick now adding to the magic of Christmas may well have served in the reign of King George the First.

Well before Christmas we children began to collect empty cotton-reels to make our own candle-holders for the Christmas table. The reels were small, slender-waisted wooden ones which are never seen today. We glued them together in columns of three and enamelled them in bright colours. They made ideal holders for the little spiral coloured candles that are still sold, and looked very pretty. We also collected six or more of the stout wooden reels on which linen thread was usually wound. Enamelled bright red with green bands, with a sprig of suitable greenery stuck in the little 'barrel', we had attractive miniature Christmas Trees for table decoration.

A great many people confess to believing that thirteen is an unlucky number, and only a tactless hostess would attempt to seat thirteen guests at the same table, especially at Christmas. This is because Judas Iscariot, who betrayed Christ, was the thirteenth disciple at the Last Supper, and nobody likes to be a Judas and one of thirteen.

A touching story of a child's concern for others has come to light, and seems appropriate to relate at the Christmas season. It happened in Laurencekirk many years ago. A school teacher was telling her class the story of the Nativity, how Mary and Joseph had nowhere to go, and how Jesus was born in a stable. One little fellow appeared deeply concerned, and a few days later came to his teacher and said, 'Please, Miss, is there ony word o' those folk gettin' a hoose?'

In Scotland it has been long the custom for townsfolk to gather at some traditional meeting-place, such as the Town Hall or the Market Cross, to welcome in the New Year; when the clock struck the midnight hour and the bells pealed out, there was much hand-shaking, back-slapping, exchanging greetings, and probably the singing of 'Auld Lang Syne' (*never* 'Old Lang Zyne') or a verse of 'A Guid New Year to ane an' a' '; then the young folk would set out on a round of First Footing.

In country places like the Glen the year drew to its close with a friendly exchange of visits and greetings at Hogmanay. In homes all over Scotland the older members of the family sat round the fire awaiting the coming of the First Foot, the customary dark man bearing gifts representing Plenty — Fuel, Food and Drink in the New Year. By tradition he had to be a bona fide visitor, a friend of the family, not a stranger.

The date of New Year's Day has been changed often, varying from November in early Celtic times to March up to the year 1600; but when it was changed to January the First that brought the old Yule Day within the Twelve Days of Christmas, and the feasting and fun and games associated with Twelfth Night were gradually transferred to Hogmanay, that is, New Year's Eve. The meaning of the word Hogmanay is obscure; some say it is of Gaelic origin, others say it has a French derivation, and others claim it is from the Greek word meaning Holy Month. Whatever its origin, Hogmanay is clearly a festival of renewal, satisfying a human need and desire to make a fresh start; hence the old Scots custom of a general tidying up of the house, the paying of bills, and the making of resolutions. Hogmanay is still Midwinter, and yet it is a time of hope and faith calling for fresh endeavour.

At the first mention of a blast o' January win' Scots the world over turn their thoughts to Robert Burns. They cele-brate his birthday, re-discover his poetry, and revive oft-repeated stories of his life and loves. He becomes again the folk hero of the nation, the prophet honoured in his own country.

I know a lady who has her great-grandfather's diary, and in it he describes how his great-great-aunt, a farmer's daughter in Dumfriesshire, when she was a girl, saw a young man leaning on the gate looking around him one summer morn-ing. She brought him to the summer-house in the garden, fetched him a glass of milk from the dairy, and in the course of conversation discovered she was entertaining the poet Burns. The diary, unfortunately, gives no account of the actual conversation, but records the sad fact that he promised to look in the next time he passed that way — and he never came back! She must have been a *very* plain young woman! Not that all Burns's heroines were beauties, but given a bright eye and a nimble wit, all other charms were added unto them from the wealth of his imagination. His sister, Mrs Begg, once said, 'Robin had aye an awfu' wark wi' the lassies. I dinna ken what he sees in them . . . I prefer a lad to the hale lot o' them.' From my parents I learned most of what I know of Robert Burns. My mother instilled in me a love of his finest songs; from my father I heard the story of his early privations, his life and times, and the women who really moulded and inspired him.

There was his mother, with her undaunted maternal spirit, and her never failing store of old ballads and songs on which her son must have fed in boyhood; there was the old relative who lived with them and helped with the carding and spinning. She was brimful of folk-lore, tales of heroic deeds and great events which fired his imagination.

We like to remember that he read to his wife nearly every line he wrote; he valued her opinion and admitted frankly that he profited by her judgment. When he was writing verses to set to traditional airs, Jean, in her sweet soprano, sang them over and over to hear how words and music suited each other. Robbie was very proud of his wife and liked to see her well-dressed. She was the first woman in Dumfries to wear a gingham gown — and gingham gowns were then in the very height of fashion, as indeed they have been once again in recent times.

It was a romantic old lady of ninety who provided the poet with his most entertaining experience. He was touring Scotland with his friend, Dr Adair, and one evening came to Clackmannan Tower, where lived a lady who claimed descent from King Robert the Bruce and treasured the sword which he had wielded at the Battle of Bannockburn. She took a great liking to Burns and his friend, invited them to dinner, and engaged them in animated conversation. After dinner she declared her intention of conferring on them the honour of knighthood, thus taking upon herself the prerogative to exercise the right of sovereignty pertaining to the heir of the old Reigning House of Scotland. She made them kneel, and in truly regal fashion, touched each lightly on the shoulder with Bruce's sword, and commanded them, 'Arise, Sir Knight!' On leaving, Burns was about to kiss the old lady's hand, but she, with a twinkle in her eye, asked, 'What ails ye at my lips, Robin?'

And he gallantly complied with her invitation.

The great January gale of 1968 went down in north-east annals as the most fearsome natural disaster in living memory. Every event thereafter was dated from The Storm. It began as a low whining noise which gradually worked up to a howl, then to a frenzied shriek. By midnight it was a gigantic unceasing buffeting, a rattling of windows and a pounding at doors. Nothing could be heard above the universal howling. Frightened folk dared not go out-of-doors lest they be blown away.

My son, Mark, a doctor in Aberdeen, was caught in the storm and could not stand upright owing to the gale force. In order to reach home he had to crawl on hands and knees.

Not only buildings suffered damage in that storm; whole forests were destroyed, great trees uprooted. It took many years to clear the woods and hillsides of fallen trees; the whole of the country suffered a devastating loss of timber.

In my childhood when the thaw came, foretelling the end of winter and the coming of spring, snow began to melt on the hill-tops, the burns came to life with a roar, born of a thousand tiny streams in the remote corries of Ben A'an, the Gairn, swollen and angry, filled the Glen with its noise. The peat-brown river surged down the valley, overflowing its banks and leaving debris in the fields, broken branches and a tangle of uprooted saplings and broom bushes. Then one morning we would wake to see only remnants of snow on the dark brown hills; in the pale glow of early sunshine and a clear blue sky above, our hearts would be lighter because the time of the singing of birds had come.

# X
# The Sweet o' the Year

When birds do sing,
hey ding-a-ding-a-ding
Shakespeare

When Scotland's spring came in over the Atlantic, sweeping across the islands of the Hebrides, it brought us respite from the protracted isolation of winter.

When the grey clouds lifted, the edge of the icy wind was noticeably blunted. Almost imperceptibly spring came to the pine woods. The massive trunks of the trees stood up rugged and strong, with, as yet, no sign of life in the rough bark, but underneath the sap was rising, and on the tops of the branches a lighter green was beginning to show. Later the new growth could be clearly seen.

The delicate fragile petals of the lovely wood sorrel brightened the mossy tops of long-fallen branches, and crept between the big stones. The smaller flowers folded up completely when the sun was hidden and at dusk. The taste of the leaves reminded us that this common little plant used to be much appreciated in salads.

Young birches had grown up in the more open parts of the woods, and on the lower slopes of Geallaig. Sown by the birds, young rowan trees appeared in profusion. The light green of the larches stood out in sharp contrast to the darker green of the pines.

Tiny ferns were shooting up all over the woods. Soon the Glen would be studded with wild flowers; daily the crocuses speared their way through the frosted grass in front of the Manse, bursting in clusters of artless beauty, yellow, purple, and white, and with the fragile snowdrop not only pleased the eye but lifted our hearts at the end of the weary winter.

March was not always a boisterous roaring month with the tree-tops bending in the rushing wind; often the weather was borrowed from April, with blue skies, white clouds and sunshine. Spring was always an exciting time. There was so much to do everywhere — spring-cleaning for housewives; and home gardeners like my father, who had been dreaming over seedsmen's catalogues for months, felt the call to action, with spade, and rake and seed-packets.

In the Glen spring came to the farmer on the first day the land was fit for working. There was a fever of sowing and growing. Behind slow-moving horses the ploughshare bit deep into the brown soil, and from the farmhouse porch, built facing away from the prevailing wind, the ever-busy farmer's wife might snatch a moment to watch, and heave a thankful sigh that the spring ploughing had at last begun.

One of the biggest changes on Gairnside — indeed in the whole countryside — is the disappearance of horses from the farms; with their departure the whole scene has changed.

When a townsman remarked to a ploughman on the fine appearance of his horses, my father overheard the tired man reply: 'Fan ye've traivelled ahint their backsides ae day efter anither, frae morn til nicht, weet an' dry, ye dinna fash yersel' gin they're bonnie or no'.'

Six hours a day, with stops at the turn of every furrow, were thought to be as much as a horse was fit for, but not for a man; when his horses were fed and stabled there was still plenty for him to do till darkness fell. One could always tell a ploughman; he walked in a sort of lop-sided manner through having to walk all his working life with one foot in the furrow and the other on top of it, bearing down on one side of the plough to keep the coulter in line with the share.

Meantime, the keeper and his helpers had progressed with the old practice of muir-burning, which dates back to the reign of King Robert III. They had to start as soon as a few windy days had dried out the surface of the hill, and had to finish by mid-April, if possible, because grouse and other moorland birds were then beginning to choose their nesting-places. Muir-burning was hard work, for the fire had to be kept under control within the selected stretch. Once out of control it might spread for miles, and beating it out was an exhausting business.

Rooks gathered in their rookeries and began to rebuild last season's nests. Each pair was very particular about its own nest, and seemed to identify every twig. Sometimes a rook would steal a twig from another nest when the rightful owners were absent. The theft was soon discovered; there was a great rumpus and much cawing and scolding until the missing stick was found. The thief knew that he had broken the law of the rookery and offered no resistance; when the stick was reclaimed the cawing died down and the interrupted nest-building was resumed.

The peeweets were tumbling in frenzied flight over the fields, and bustling about looking after their chicks. If anything frightened the mother she gave the command to the

133

chicks to lie low. She herself did all she could to lead the danger away; if it was an inquisitive collie that caused the alarm the mother peeweet would flap along the ground pretending she had a broken wing, and tempt the collie away to follow her.

We welcomed the cuckoo, but to the little birds who would be victimised the sound he made was far from welcome. They knew him as their enemy and would boldly attack him; he always turned tail and flew away from his small assailant, but he did not go far. The female cuckoo waited close by to see where a nest was being built, then, choosing her time, laid an egg in it.

Corncrakes were numerous then, shy birds skulking in long grass. We never actually saw them but heard their harsh grating cry through the night in distant fields.

There were hosts of birds in the woods; the friendly little chaffinch, wood pigeons who built their nests high in the spruces, and, if disturbed, would flit among the trees, the sound of their wings like a clap of castanets. There were herons by the river. We saw them in flight when they returned from their wandering to the heronry in spring. Near the edge of the Delnabo wood where capercailzies came to build their nests, we sometimes caught a glimpse of the long-billed woodcock as it twisted among the pines.

Glen Gairn was a fine place for birds throughout the year; where e'er we walked there were birds, whatever the season, whatever the time of day, in the woods, by the river, in the open fields, and on the heathery hills.

In the poems we were taught at school, we learned that spring was heralded by the coming of the swallow and the first notes of the cuckoo. We accepted that that might be so in the sunny south, but we knew the end of winter had come when we heard the cry of the oyster-catcher and were overjoyed to see a number of them with their orange-red bills and boldly pied plumage flying low over the Gairn. These interesting birds, traditionally associated with the sea-shore, in north-east Scotland have long bred inland.

By late March plovers were wheeling and tossing, and calling over the ploughed fields, and whaups thrilling the air over the moors with their wild spring song. When they heard the haunting sound with all the mystery of the lonely moors in its eerie cry, old men shivered and said it was uncanny.

The martins came in late spring, after their long journey across the Alps from their winter holiday in Africa. They were joined by screaming swifts who came to build their nests under the eaves of the old Manse barn, to raise their young on the plentiful summer insects which they took on the wing.

We noticed the days grow longer and although easterly winds often blew strong and cold we felt that with the approach of April even the hedgehogs could end their hibernation and come out to enjoy the sunshine. We sometimes saw one in an evening down the side of a dyke on a slug or beetle hunt. There were exceptions to that nocturnal wandering for food. We often spotted one in broad daylight after a heavy downpour, which brought slugs and snails out of the freshly soaked greenery.

The last tree in the woods to hear the call of spring was the ash. In April it still stood as it did in midwinter with its bare branches looking skywards.

The gean trees by the west wall in the Manse garden, were surpassingly lovely in their spring-time dress, a mass of delicate white blossom, decked as if for a wedding, bridal and beautiful.

Occasionally, at the foot of a hedge we might spot the late-flowering golden heads of coltsfoot, which, in the south, are considered the true harbingers of spring. The leaves, which only appear long after the plant has ceased flowering, were gathered by country-women long ago, dried, and smoked in a short clay pipe to relieve asthma.

The modest little daisy, the 'day's eye', has always been beloved of poets, from Chaucer, who said it was his favourite wild flower, to Robert Burns, who apologised to the crimson-tipped flower when he uprooted it with his plough. An old name for the daisy was Herb Margaret, which meant either a pearl or a daisy. In John Wycliffe's version of the Bible, he actually says 'Neither cast ye your margarites before swine'. Monks dedicated the daisy to Saint Margaret, wife of King Malcolm III of Scotland. She re-built the monastery of Iona, and was canonised in 1251 for her great benefactions to the church.

Many eminent women wore the daisy as their personal symbol. The Lady Margaret, mother of King Henry VIII, had three white daisies as her special device; Margaret of Anjou had daisies embroidered on the robes of her courtiers, and made her ladies wear them in their hair. And my grand-daughter Marguerite carried a posy of marguerites on her wedding-day, and had them embroidered on her train!

At the first sign of daffodils in the Manse garden we were ready at the drop of a hat to quote William Wordsworth who wandered lonely as a cloud and was cheered by the sight of a host of golden daffodils. Ours were like the early flowers of Shakespeare's day, small, slender, short-stemmed flowers, growing only a few inches above the ground, on the grassy banks under the currant bushes, but in a lively wind they tossed and nodded, as if they would shake off their little golden heads.

In May the hawthorn was heavy with blossom, and though many people for some superstitious reason will not have it brought into their homes, we thought the white flowers were specially welcome and smelled delicious. We laughed at all superstition; what, we asked, is the matter with the month of May? In that month, according to the extra-wary, we must not eat oysters (not that we had much chance of doing that in Glen Gairn), we must not cast a clout, nor marry, nor must the cat have kittens, but for lasting beauty, one should wash one's face in May Morning Dew.

May brought fresh colour to the Glen; it was good to see blue skies feathered with airy clouds and to see the birchwoods touched with green again. It was a time of bird song, blossom, and bumble bees. Kingcups shone on the marshy banks of the little burn that wandered slowly past Stranlea. The birds were clamorous. Blackbirds alternately fluted and scolded as they bustled about in search of food for their nestlings. There were yellow discs of coltsfoot to be seen, and a sprinkling of gold could also be seen where the lesser celandine spread her shining flowerets in the warm sunshine.

The woods round the Manse held magic for Ellie and me; they were full of secret hiding-places and wild flowers in plenty. First came the wood-anemones, sometimes called wind-flowers because they always turn away from the prevailing wind; the pinky-white of their drooping bell-like flowers were tinged with purple on the outside. Their roots crept along close to the surface of the ground, and we were very careful not to pick the flowers carelessly lest the whole plant came away in our hands. We noticed a few glistening flowers of the yellow celandine, for they opened their glossy petals early in spring, but these tiny flowers were always at their best in May.

We found masses of dog's mercury, followed by the pussy willow. Robert Neil, the brilliant son of my father's predecessor, identified over eighty species of willow in the Glen.

The alder trees by the waterside produced charming catkins; every tassel on the larches was coloured crimson, and every twig was laden with these cones of the future; on the spruce trees hung long tapering cones, brightly coloured in their immaturity; long shoots appeared on the pines with two knobs at the tip of each shoot, which eventually became a cone.

The cowslips which grew in profusion on the Manse brae gladdened our eyes and we looked forward to their appearance year after year. We gathered huge bunches and made cowslip balls by picking off the heads as close to the top of the main stem as possible. We then hung fifty or sixty of them on a long string stretched between two chairs placed back to back. We pressed the flower heads carefully together and tied the string tightly to gather them into a pretty ball. They were fragile playthings for an hour. Elizabeth Barrett Browning refers to this childish ploy in the lines

> Many tender souls
> have strung their losses on a rhyming thread
> as children cowslips; the more pains they take
> The work more withers.

Hay-making was a busy time for the farmers in the Glen. The whole family, and neighbours, helped to get the hay in safe and dry. Children loved to ride on the horse-drawn cart piled high with hay to the stackyard or to a corner of the hay-field. There it was built into a loaf-shaped stack called a 'soo' which was laid on a foundation of brushwood and built high in the middle, so that the hay would slope downward from the centre all round and so keep rain from soaking and rotting it.

Like Oliver Goldsmith I love everything that is old – 'old friends, old times, old manners, old books, old wines' and in my day have collected, as well as horse brasses, such varied articles as curling tongs, goffering irons, flat irons (which occasionally function as book-ends), glove stretchers, and eye-baths made of blue and amber glass.

I have retained my interest in moustache cups, such as my father used. All are beautifully decorated with floral designs, and complete with matching saucers, no two are alike. I also collect feeding-cups of the once-familiar type – with a spout like a teapot, a handle like a cup, and a built-in shelf to prevent the spilling of liquid when placing the spout between the lips of a recumbent patient. The prettily-decorated cups would be found in a patient's bedroom, the plain cups were probably used in hospitals where, I understand, many have now been replaced by disposable beakers and straws.

I possess a number of an earlier design, like a shallow sauce-boat in shape without an extended spout or handle. I am now trying to collect some of the old-time shaving mugs. In the days of the cut-throat razor a shaving mug was a necessity, with a perforated shallow shelf on which the soapy shaving-brush rested and dripped into the deep cup.

I have a very satisfying collection of drinking mugs, old and modern, each with a history. It includes beakers, cups and saucers, and other items which commemorate Jubilees, Coronations, and similar royal occasions from Victoria's day, and even the Coronation that never was – that of King Edward VIII.

I collected cruisies at one time. Now I have only one left, but the others provide a talking-point in the homes of the friends to whom I gave them. Blacksmith-made, they hung at cottage firesides – primitive lamps, which were also used in barns, byres and stables, with mutton fat or fish oil and a peeled rash for a wick. The rashes were gathered when the moon was full as they were said to be at their best then; peeling the rashes for wicks was generally done by the children. My cruisie, typical of its day, consists of two leaf-shaped wrought-iron pans, one above the other, the upper one fixed on a ratchet so that it could be made to tilt forward when necessary to use every drop of the oil in the pan in which the wick floated.

My treasures are not shut up in cupboards. They contribute to the atmosphere and character of a room — a quaich supports a cactus plant, a mug holds a posy, my great-uncle's tureen (mended with rivets as was done in days before china could be invisibly mended) sits in the hearth crammed with giant cones gathered in a wood in Normandy, and my grandmother's brass tea-kettle keeps it company.

One of the signs of the disappearance of horses from the streets and on farms is the frequent appearance in small antique shops and auction sale-rooms of horse brasses — martingales, fly terrets, fliers, or swingers, name-plates, face pieces, and 'broo ban's'. They were originally intended to ward off the evil eye. Polished brass, flashing as the horse moved, was supposed to distract the Devil and destroy his power. The Romans introduced them to Britain. They decorated their horses' harness with amulets of polished bronze to represent the sun god, the guardian of driven horses. Amulets must have been worn at a very early date, for they are even mentioned in the Old Testament. In Judges we read of crescents like the moon on camels' necks; and Isaiah warns Jewish women that their amulets will be taken from them, because they were symbols of the Horns of Isis, and of Diana, the goddess of horses. The earliest types are of plain circular or crescent shapes, followed by many geometrical designs based on the rays of the sun, also lily and lotus flowers, showing Greek and Egyptian influence.

Older brasses were fashioned by hand from brass sheets, and later from rolled brass. After 1830 most of them were cast in moulds, or machine-stamped. In early and mid-Victorian times they were designed to associate with a purchaser's district or trade. The ploughman could have his plough, the carter his wheatsheaf, the circus could have an elephant, and brewers could have a barrel.

For the Coronation of Queen Victoria in 1838, cast face pieces were issued showing the Queen's portrait. Late-nineteenth-century brasses included portraits of politicians; twentieth-century designs include Shakespeare, Lincoln, Nelson, Wellington, Robert Burns, and more recently, Winston Churchill. There are private and county crests, Masonic and heraldic designs, a multitude of horse designs including hunters and race horses. There is even one of a carter who is evidently asleep for he is leaning with his back to the plodding horse. There are Manx cats, railway engines, and ships at sea, and thousands more.

Once I owned over two hundred brasses and had an ideal setting for them. I collected them over the years before collectors had begun to find it an interesting hobby. I used to take a selection with me when, by invitation, I attended meetings of various women's organisations, and some men's clubs, to talk about them, and explain their origin and the meaning of each design. I never submitted an article on the subject to an editor, but I knew a collector who did; he borrowed some of my brasses to illustrate the published article, but omitted to mention the source!

There came a time when I realised that the amount of time entailed in keeping my collection brightly polished could be more usefully spent. They are all scattered now.

The hills, the woods, the meadows are part of our natural heritage, and to desecrate them by the wholesale uprooting of plants, the destruction of birds and the robbing of their nests, is to deprive not only ourselves but others of the lasting pleasure and peace that can only be found in the unspoiled countryside. Brought up as I was close to the soil, I have retained the mental background of tilled fields, green trees and wide skies. I am keenly aware of the debt I owe to my country up-bringing. Time and time again my thoughts have turned in troubled times to the blessed peace of those early years, and I have always found in the remembered fragrance of woodlands after rain, and the smell of a newly-ploughed field, a miraculous something that refreshes and revives the spirit.

# XI
# Prestonfield Revisited

> 'Twas within a mile o' Edinburgh town
> In the rosy time o' the year.
>
> D'Urfey

At the base of Arthur's Seat, half a mile from Duddingston Loch, stands Prestonfield House, in its own broad acres, not far from the Palace of Holyroodhouse. Shadows of trees as old as the seventeenth-century house trace their pattern across its harled walls; a Scots pine, symbol of Jacobite refuge from pursuing redcoats, stands near the front door.

Peacocks step with dignity across the paths, secure in the knowledge that it is all their own, while pheasants and partridges feed fearlessly on the lawn — and all within the limits of the City of Edinburgh.

I have pleasant memories of my first visit to Prestonfield, on a March evening in 1973, when my publishers gave a party to launch my first book, *The Hills of Home*. I was happy to meet at last my friends from London with whom I had corresponded for over a year, and who, I discovered, had already marked the occasion of their visit to Edinburgh by climbing Arthur's Seat. They were much impressed by the view from the top, and with the Castle set high on its precipice with Scotland's history in every grey stone, looking across the Firth of Forth to the dreaming hills of Fife.

Among the guests at the party were booksellers, book critics, and librarians, poets, essayists, novelists, and Routledge authors, journalists, and personal friends, among them members of my own family. I was proud to stand with my hosts at the head of the wide staircase to welcome each guest on arrival.

Prestonfield House has a most interesting history. It is first recorded in a Royal Charter of 1153 when it was granted to the monks of Harehope in Northumberland. In 1164, King David II of Scotland, after eleven years of captivity in England, withdrew the grant because the monks had supported his enemy, Edward III, and Prestfield, as it was then called, reverted to the Scottish Crown. Successive owners held it in fee for a pair of gloves rendered annually on St Giles's Day.

William Dick of Braid, who lent King James I the sum of six thousand pounds to defray the expenses of his journey to Scotland, was the greatest of the old Edinburgh merchants, with fleets of ships extending from the Baltic to the Mediterranean, but he was reduced to poverty and died in a debtor's prison. Because he was a well-known Royalist, and advanced large sums in favour of the Scots Government in the time of Charles II, he provoked the wrath of the English Commonwealth, and was ruined by the heavy fines he had to pay the English. Poor Sir William! (He had been created a baronet by Charles I.) He went to London to try to recover part of his lost wealth and was mockingly told that surely he, by means of the Philosopher's Stone, could get pie-crust when less fortunate people could get bread.*

Sir William died in Westminster Prison. There is a picture in Prestonfield House which shows him there, poorly clad, surrounded by his hapless family. His grandson, Sir James, acquired the property from Sir Thomas Hamilton, and restored the family fortunes, which were founded on the sale of manure swept off Edinburgh streets on the understanding that for a certain number of years he would be allowed to remove it free of charge.

Sir James was a staunch supporter of the Roman Catholic interest, and in 1680 was summoned to London by Charles II to attend his brother James, Duke of York. James's political ineptitude made him a liability to his hard-pressed brother, so he was sent over the Border, and came to live at the Palace of Holyroodhouse, where his next-door neighbour was Sir James Dick. A close friendship developed between the two men; the Duke, who later became King James II, was a frequent visitor at Prestonfield, often arriving on foot by a path from the Palace, which came to be known as the Duke's Walk. Sir James was at the time Lord Provost of the City of Edinburgh, much battered by the religious storms of the age, and his friendship with the Heir to the Throne brought him nothing but universal disapproval on both religious and political grounds.

The students of Edinburgh University in the 'No Popery' riot of 1681, thwarted in their desire to burn an effigy of the Pope, burned Prestonfield House instead. The Duke of

*According to legend, Noah was commanded to hang up the genuine Philosopher's Stone in the Ark to give light there to every living creature. Many discoveries, which brought wealth, were made in past centuries by people who had been seeking the Stone, so mention of it came to mean a way to wealth.

York tried to make amends by re-building it, but the state of the Treasury was low, and no more than £800 was ever received by Sir James for this purpose. Yet rebuild it he did, in the form, designed by the celebrated Sir William Bruce of Kinross, in which it remains to this day.

When Sir James died in 1728 he was succeeded by his daugher Janet. Her son was Sir Alexander Dick, an eminent physician and an intimate friend of Dr Samuel Johnson. In 1745 Sir Alexander received at Prestonfield Prince Charles Edward, the ill-fated Bonnie Prince Charlie. One document alone survives to bear witness to the troubled events of 1745 and 1746; it is a receipt for £100 for the Prince's use. Another guest at Prestonfield was Benjamin Franklin who later became American Ambassador to the Court of Louis XVI, when, in 1778, France entered the War of Independence against the English.

James Boswell was also a frequent visitor, and on 19 November 1778, in the company of Dr Samuel Johnson, he dined at Prestonfield. The two guests had just returned from their tour of the Western Isles of Scotland, and were entertained in the Tapestry Room. That night Sir Alexander, who took a practical interest in the production of rhubarb for table use, noted in his diary, 'I gave Dr. Johnson rhubarb seeds and some melon.'

It is of interest to recall that another Scot, Dr James Mounsey, was a Royal Physician in Tsarist Russia and a leading Army doctor. When he returned to Scotland he brought with him the first seeds of the true rhubarb to reach this country. This was the medicinal rhubarb, not the variety which now grows in our gardens. It was the basis for Dr Gregory's Powder, that nauseous mixture which was mercilessly administered to luckless children in great-grandmother's day. The Society for the Encouragement of Arts and

Commerce considered the introduction of these seeds to be of such importance that a special gold medal was struck to honour Dr James Mounsey. He died in Edinburgh in 1773.

Six years later that same Society awarded Sir Alexander Dick a similar gold medal for producing the best specimen of British rhubarb.

My daughter Elspeth and I toured the house, ascending and descending the old stone stairs, every step worn and hollowed by the feet of notable people who stayed there down the centuries. At every step I reminded myself that the feet of Dr Samuel Johnson had actually trod these very stairs.

Having admired the Tapestry Room and the smaller Leather Room with its unique panels which were bought in Cordova in 1676, we came to the lovely Italian Room, panelled with seventeenth-century Flemish paintings, and in the Blue Room saw landscapes by nineteenth-century painters.

We examined the Visitors' Book containing signatures of ambassadors, opera singers, gourmets from every State of the Union, and addresses that read like a World Gazetteer.

A direct descendant of that Sir James Dick who acquired Prestonfield in 1677 still keeps close contact with the home of his ancestors, and it remains effectively alive as a country house, escaping the metamorphosis into a museum, which afflicts some of its contemporaries.

# XII
# The Howe o' the Mearns Again

We will take the good old way,
We'll take and keep the good old way.
Translated from the Gaelic by
the Rev. A. Stewart, LLD

A few lines in an Angus newspaper have brought my father's early diaries vividly to mind — briefly, it appears that 'they' are going to create a picnic area on Garvock Hill.

How often my father, in his youthful days in Laurencekirk, wrote in his careful hand 'my brother and I went up the hill'. No need the name the brother or the hill — for him, and Tom, his youngest brother and close companion, Garvock Hill was a favourite evening climb. The boys, I believe, came to regard it as their own territory, for few showed any inclination to share the climb, the summit, and the magnificent view. Today it is the haunt of hill-walkers who rest a while at the top while they enjoy the unspoiled panorama — woods of beech and pine, spires delicate and distant, far-off hills etched faintly on the azure of the northern sky.

Laurencekirk, with rich farmland on all sides, its fertile red soil so characteristic of the district, lies at the very heart of the Howe O' The Mearns. It had its beginning many centuries ago when it was known as Kirktoon of Conveth, and later was named after Saint Laurence, who visited the Mearns in the year 605.

The Johnston Tower, that well-loved landmark overlooking the town, was built by James Farquhar of Johnston in the early nineteenth century.

Modern Laurencekirk owes much to Francis Garden, who became Lord Gardenstone. When he acquired the Johnston Estate he devoted his life to the welfare of Laurencekirk. He encouraged the building of houses and introduced cottage industries — spinning, weaving, and bleaching. He secured a Charter in 1779, raising the village to the status of a burgh which gave it the privilege of holding the weekly market which has continued to this day. In 1791 Lord Gardenstone erected the second Kirk of Saint Laurence, the first having been burned down by the Duke of Cumberland's men in 1745. This kirk survived till 1872, when it was replaced by the kirk of today.

On the site of a small inn known as the Boar's Head Lord Gardenstone built the Gardenstone Arms, which still thrives. A notable visitor to the Boar's Head was Robert Burns, who presented the innkeeper with a volume of his poems, and described his wife as 'jolly, frank, sensible, and love-inspiring'.

In these days of industrial strife it is pleasant to look back on the contented days of the hand-loom weavers. In the late eighteenth century in villages in the Mearns every man had a loom, and in addition had a croft and kept a cow. All the weaving was done by the father and sons, the spinning by the mother and daughters. The whole family helped with the crops and in the cutting and stacking of peats in summer, to give the household winter warmth.

In Laurencekirk today one looks in vain for anyone who takes snuff, yet at one time this town in the Howe O' the Mearns was renowned for the making of snuff-boxes, a craft begun by Charles Stiven, a Glenbervie man, in 1783. He, head of the family firm, became widely known as the Prince of Snuff-Mull Makers. These were made in goat's horn, ram's horn, and in wood, and were usually embellished with paintings or carving; but for fine craftsmanship none could compare with those made by the Stivens, a special feature of their own 'Laurencekirk Snuff-Mull' being a concealed hinge and wooden pin, Charles' invention. In those days, snuff-mulls and tobacco-jars had their place in every home and nearly everybody, including women, took snuff.

Snuff-taking was the hallmark of the medical profession, and many virtues were ascribed to this powdered form of tobacco. Some snuff-takers had a waistcoat-pocket lined with leather. This they filled with snuff each morning. Throughout the day the owner's thumb and forefinger would be constantly diving into it.

Examples of these cleverly-made and beautifully decorated mulls are now highly prized. There are fine examples of these boxes in the Folk Museum at Glamis. The enterprising and hard-working Stiven family produced many other articles, both useful and ornamental, including a steady supply of teetotums priced at a ha'penny for the children.

My father used to make miniature tops from cotton-reels for my sister and me when we were very small. He called them 'peeries' and made them 'birl like a teetotum'.

The teetotum of Stiven's creation was a little gambling device of the once popular Put and Take variety, actually of

Roman origin. On its four sides it showed in Roman capitals the letters A, D, N and T, which stood for

> Accipe unum,
> Donato alium,
> Nihil, and
> Totum.

Luck depended on which of the four sides lay uppermost when the totum stopped birling. My father and his brothers and the other youngsters did not use the Latin terms; what they shouted when the totum birled to a standstill was

> A — take ane,
> D — duntle doon ane,
> N — nickie naethin', — or triumphantly,
> T — tak' a'!

As children they were taken in farm-carts to the Clatterin' Brig for their annual Sunday School Picnic. It's a pleasant-sounding name, Clatterin' Brig. It makes one think of horse-drawn carts rumbling and clattering as they journey across a rustic bridge. Yet the name has nothing to do with cart-wheels; in its Gaelic form it was clacharan, meaning stepping stones. Folk who travelled that way on foot used the stones to cross the burn while horses and carts splashed through a shallow ford. To this day, this charming little nook in the quiet braes of the Mearns is a favourite picnic spot for motorists.

Clatterin' Brig's real claim to fame, however, is its being the starting point of the historic Cairn o' Mounth hill road. The road climbs at a steep gradient from 400 feet to 1,400 feet in the space of two miles. Then, after crossing the high moors, it descends as steeply towards Glen Dye and Royal Deeside, and is well known for being so often reported blocked by snow. On a clear day the view from the summit is magnificent.

My father, I recall, had a number of minor idiosyncracies of speech which I assume were survivals of the accent of his Angus boyhood. In reciting the alphabet to us children he slurred over the letter W as 'dub-you', and prolonged Z to 'izz-zed'. He referred to his clerical collars as 'cullers', and to the cuckoo as the 'cuck-oo'.

True to his beloved classics, to the end of his life he continued to speak of the cinema as the kinema, sound in his belief that the origin of the word demanded a hard 'c'. He was proud to recall that the Mearns had produced a number of notable people, including James Beattie, the eminent Scots poet, who was born in Laurencekirk in 1735, and was Professor of Philosophy in Marischal College, Aberdeen; Robert William Thomson, the brilliant civil engineer and inventor of the pneumatic tyre, was born at Stonehaven in 1822; Hercules Linton, designer of the *Cutty Sark*, that far-famed clipper, was born at Inverbervie in 1836; and the famous Scots violinist, J. Scott Skinner, composer of many strathspeys and reels, was born at Banchory in 1843. In more recent times, it was at Drumlithie that James Leslie Mitchell was born in 1901, and brought up on his father's farm. He wrote under the name of Lewis Grassic Gibbon and in 1932 published the first of his trilogy, *Sunset Song*, followed by *Cloud Howe* and *Grey Granite* which, under the title *A Scots Quair*, became a classic, immortalising the lives of folk in the Mearns in the early 1900s.

My grandmother, who spent all her married life in Laurencekirk, often spoke of her happy childhood near Lunan Bay with its magnificent three-mile strand and dunes, and the crumbling walls of Red Castle, still standing guard over the south of the river. The Lunan Water runs through some of the pleasantest country in Angus and is the happy hunting ground for trout fishers and bird-watchers. J.B. Salmond featured the Lunan Water and the surrounding district in his novel *The Toby Jug*.

The oldest part of the Castle, a massive fragment of wall, was almost certainly built more than eight hundred years ago. The colour of the stone gave it the name of Red Castle from the earliest days. In a deed dated 1286 it bears that name.

The Kirk of Lunan, where my grandmother worshipped with her parents and brothers, will always be associated with that brave man, Walter Myln, whose name is the last inscribed on the Martyrs' Monument in St Andrews where he suffered death rather than give up his religious beliefs. 'You will know', he said, 'that I will not recant the truth, for I am corn and not chaff. I will not be blown away by the wind.' There are unusual brass ornaments in Lunan Kirk; one is a support for the font, the other is a stand for the hour-glass. They were given to the kirk by a former beadle. One of his duties had been to turn the sand-glass during the sermon to remind the minister and the congregation of the passing of time.

Some years ago my daughter Elspeth took my cousin Alison (Tom's daughter) and me to visit Muir of Lunan, the former home of our great-grandparents, which still stands, a solid, stone-built house, its exterior unchanged down the years, and still occupied.

My grandmother, in spite of her endless household tasks and the care of her numerous children, was a happy woman, because her home was her world — looking after her husband and family her one absorbing interest — yet her outlook was not narrow. Having four brothers in the ministry she was ambitious for her sons and wished them to follow in their uncles' footsteps, and was very proud when they did. Her daughters, however, had to stay at home, and take their share of the unending procession of duties that were considered to be women's work. The boys cleaned their boots, fed the pig and did outdoor work on the farm; the girls did all the indoor work, including washing and ironing for the whole family, and learned to become very proficient needlewomen. That was the traditional pattern for bringing up children in large families in those days; the boys had their recognised routine jobs, and the girls did everything else. My grandmother, with the ordeal of fourteen births behind her, knew that a woman had to be clever and smile inwardly when referred to as the weaker sex.

What better way to finish this story than to borrow from the pages of my Commonplace Book the wisdom of a woman who, long years ago, prayed

Lord, Thou knowest that I am growing old;
keep me from getting talkative, and from the fatal habit
    of thinking
that I must say *something* on every subject on every
    occasion.
Release me from craving to try to straighten out
    everybody's affairs.
Give me grace to listen to the story of others' pains . . .
help me to endure them with patience, but seal my lips
    on my own aches and pains . . .
ever increasing, and my love of rehearsing them grows as
    the years go by.
Keep my mind free from the recital of endless details . . .
give me wings to get to the point.
Teach me the glorious lesson that it *is* possible I may

occasionally be mistaken.
Keep me reasonably sweet;
I don't want to be a saint (some of them are *so* hard to
    live with)
but a sour old woman is one of the crowning works of
    the Devil.
Make me thoughtful, but not moody;
helpful, but not bossy.
With my vast store of wisdom it seems a pity not to
    use it all,
but Thou knowest, Lord, that I want a few friends at
    the end.

# Some Books Consulted

Bassin, Ethel, *The Old Songs of Skye: Frances Tolmie and her Circle*, Routledge & Kegan Paul, 1977.

Gaffney, Victor, *Tomintoul: Its Glens and its People*, The Sutherland Press, 1970.

Gordon, Seton, *The Cairngorm Hills of Scotland*, Cassells, 1925.

McKerrow, Janie, *In Unity*, printed privately.

MacPherson, John, *John von Lamont, Astronomer Royal*, printed privately, 1930.

Underwood, Peter, *Gazetteer of Scottish Ghosts*, Fontana, 1974.

Wyness, Fenton, *Royal Valley*, Alex P. Reid, 1968.

Young, Douglas, *Scotland*, Cassells, 1971.

# Glossary

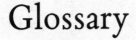

ae — one
ahint — behind
allood — allowed
anker — a measure, varying in
    different countries, up to 8½
    Imperial gallons
appleringie — southernwood
atween — between
auld — old
ava — at all
averins — cloudberries
awa — away

beadle — church officer
birling — spinning
bonnet laird — small landowner
bothy — accommodation for
    unmarried farm-workers
box-bed — bed in a recess and
    enclosed when not in use
byre — cow-house

calfie — small calf
cam — came
clachan — small hamlet

claes — clothes
coulter — turf-cutter on the stem
    or beam of a plough
couped — overturned
croft — smallholding

dinna — don't
dockit — docked, cut-off
dreich — dull

fan — when
fash yersel' — bother yourself
ferlies — fairings
forebears — ancestors

gauger — exciseman
gin — if
girdle — griddle
girnal — meal chest

harled — rough-cast
hint o' hairst — end of harvest
howe — hollow or sheltered place

kail — curly greens

# Glossary

kail-yaird — cabbage-patch
kenspeckle — easily recognised

lade — channel leading water to
 a mill
laird — landowner
langsyne — long ago
larach — the ruined foundation
 of a dwelling
linn — waterfall
lo'ed — loved
lowsin' — unyoking

morn, the — tomorrow
moss, peat — bog
mounth — mountain pass in the
 Grampians

pan drops — a hard peppermint-
 flavoured sweet
peel — pool, puddle
peeweets — lapwings
piece — a packed lunch

pirns — reels of cotton
pow — head of hair

quaich — drinking vessel

rashes — rushes
reiving — plundering

skailed — emptied
skelped — spanked
soomed — swam
soughin' — sighing

tatties — potatoes
traivelled — travelled on foot

unco — unusually

verra — very

weet — wet
whaups — curlews
whins — gorse